# MANIFEST YOUR STORY

## IN 21 DAYS

How to write a short story, novella, or novel from scratch, step by step

DANIEL HIETALA
ROBERT CAVALIERE

# Table of Contents

# Manifest a Story in 21 Days

How to Write a Short Story, Novella, or Novel from Scratch, Step by Step

**Daniel Hietala, MFA**

**Robert Cavaliere**

*"A writer writes because there is no other choice."*

Mr. Larsen, our English teacher

# Introduction

If you let go now, you will slide, fall, and hit the canyon below, crushing your bones to dust. You grasp and claw and dig your fingernails into the rusty sediment as long as you can, clinging for dear life. The problem is that your grip is loosening, your muscles are failing, and the dirt is sliding beneath you.

Maybe if you thrust your weight to the left you can reach the rock ledge jutting out four feet away and save yourself, but you lack the strength for this move. So you freeze. Your fingers give out...you fall.

As a struggling or failed writer, you have found yourself on a proverbial cliff many times, grasping at the dream of becoming an author, holding on as long as you could while each manuscript slipped away. At what point do you stop getting up? When does the writer in you die?

My literary death came in my early 30's. I hung up my figurative fedora and settled into a good life as family man and professional, no longer fighting the quiet fight to bring my writing dreams to life. It was no longer worth the time, effort, energy, and disappointment—not after a fateful phone call one night.

A family friend connected me with an editor of a publishing company to offer feedback on a few chapters of a children's chapter book I had written, but I could tell by the tone of his voice he didn't want to talk to me...or maybe I was just picking up on the fact that he thought my book was terrible. Whichever the case, his feedback was blunt: My word choice was off. My sentences were too long. I was not appealing to my target audience. After that, I really don't remember the rest of his discouraging feedback. All I knew was I was done. I was given a chance—an open door—and I blew it. Rejection equalled the death of a dream...one death too many.

That kind of disappointment can last for decades. At least it did for me. I didn't recover from the discouragement until the latter part of my forties *after* successfully raised three of our five kids with my wife (two are still at home) and having moved my way up the career ladder. Eventually, I stumbled into enough confidence to give my writing career another chance...and I'm not looking back. My co-author has never experienced a period of futility as I have. He simply didn't publish or attempt to seek out an agent for decades, which has its own effect on confidence. We have a sneaking suspicion we are not alone in the discouragement and fear that obstructed our progress as authors.

For some reason, life as a writer lends itself to disappointment, dejection, fear, self-depreciation, and isolation. Maybe these feelings are akin to the struggles of other kinds of artists when their aspirations outpace their growth and development, but writing already lends itself to self-punishment because it is an act of isolation. Except for rare instances of writing teams, a writer lives and dies (artistically) by his/her own individual efforts, whereas members of a band have their jam sessions and actors their community theater. A writer sits alone in the early hours—like me right now while the rest of the house and much of the world are asleep because I can't think or write clearly with the stress of the day breathing down my neck. While it is peaceful, it is alone—my thoughts my own cynical audience.

Even more disheartening is what I call the *man-behind-the-curtain* feeling: the fear that your reader is going to look right through your story and only see a wanna-be writer pulling levers and engineering smoke. You are attempting to be a "great and powerful wizard" of storytelling; instead, everyone sees a hack and a fake.

Maybe you don't have this imposter syndrome. Maybe you possess the right levels of motivation and confidence to write books but are discouraged by the grind of every day life—life on the hamster wheel.

You have never found a way to sustain writing while working a full-time job while simultaneously taking care of your family and responsibilities. Your schedule puts you through the wringer every day, leaving you exhausted with little to no energy for something as cognitively challenging as writing a book—something few people will ever do in their lives anyway. And when you do have a moment of relaxation, whether it's a weekend or a vacation, why would you start a book when you know you aren't going to be able sustain it during 'real' life?

First of all, that is a terrible way to live. And believe me, I get it. My life as an author was stunted by both syndromes—I felt like the man-behind-the-curtain and the hamster-on-the-wheel. Success as a husband, father, employee, and productive citizen consoled my failures as a writer, though I could not escape a muffled cry inside. After all, we are spiritual beings, and not only do we need to connect with the source of our spiritual life, writers in particular need to communicate the depths of their soul in the form of storytelling, just as a musicians needs to take up their instrument and play. We need to visit worlds that don't exist, live out lives we only dream, embark on adventures beyond all other realities.

The human spirit was never intended to simply survive. We are meant to live, thrive, love, and create. If you are a writer, you have no other choice but to make writing a centerpiece of your life.

Of course, it's easier to give up. Let go. Fall. Leave a hole behind where a writer met cold, hard reality...or you can turn your life as a writer around today. Yes, in a single day, as long as it is the first day of a new habit. Any habit can be learned given enough routine and practice—21 days being the absolute minimum to develop one. It doesn't matter how much time you spend each day writing—I usually get away with 30 to

40 minutes early in the morning. It only matters that you establish a consistent writing habit.

Don't believe us? Well, take a minute to think about the kind of habits you currently manifest. When a great idea comes to mind, what do you do? Do you discard it like any other idea or write it down? When you get the itch to write, do you stick your phone in another room and shut yourself in a quiet place to write for an hour or two? Or do you turn on the TV or flick through your phone? If you find yourself doing things instead of writing every day, it means that you have hardwired your brain to manifest a different kind of identity. While this identity may allow you to live a good life, it is not the identity of a writer, and you will rarely—if ever—manifest the stories in you.

This book will take you through a 21-day process to develop the habits of a serious writer as you complete a short story, or get a strong start on a novella or novel. But no matter how far you get in your story, the goal is to live, act, think, produce, and believe that you are a writer. By the end of 21 days, not only will you manifest a story, but you will manifest the writer inside of you.

—

There is an old saying that says, 'The road to Hell is paved with the best of intentions.' Similarly, the road to writing failure is paved with inspiration. Writers, like most artists, are emotional creatures, driven by passion and prone to diving into a creative project with blinders on while ignoring the rest of our responsibilities. Alternately, we are often predisposed to insecurity and inconsistency and can go months, if not years, ignoring the very projects we started with such passion. While we are easy to inspire, we are similarly easy to discourage.

The source of our discouragement can usually be traced back to the dynamic relationship between belief and behavior.

To get off that cliff alive, you must first *believe* you can survive whatever manuscript you are working on, or develop any story idea that has inspired you. No one can believe this for you. The problem with belief, of course, is that it cannot be faked. You can't *believe* a book into existence, or believe your stories into manifestation, which brings us back to the same problem. How do you arrive at a new belief in yourself?

While you *can* have a divine encounter, an eye-opening epiphany, or an inspirational mentor who plants a belief in yourself, most of us require a more dogged, monotonous path to belief: a change in habits.

Even if you started off with a belief in yourself as a writer, what changed? Mostly likely a pattern of poor writing habits became a poor belief about yourself...that became your identity as a failed writer...that became a self-fulfilling prophecy every time you sat down to write and gave up. Belief, after all, is downstream from behavior.

Habits not only make up our lives, they take over our lives. Entertainment, socializing, hobbies, social media, junkfood, alcohol, and sports eat our writing time for lunch. Actually, the world is content with you living in the little box of habits you have created for yourself. Alternately, if you change your habits, you change your life.

Have you noticed that no one is demanding you to write? No one is expecting you to read this book and apply its strategies to your own writing. If you are waiting for an inspirational mentor to come out of the blue and notice your potential as a writer, you're better off watching "Finding Forrester." At least you will vicariously experience the payoff of a writer's happy ending. Even more fantastical, if you are waiting for your boss to stop by your office one day and say, "You know what? You look like you could benefit from a creative outlet. Go ahead and take the last hour off every day and work on that book you've been talking about!"

No amount of tapping the heels of your Birkenstocks will make this fantasy come true. But that doesn't mean that you can't interrupt your own routine, stick your phone in a drawer and tell yourself, 'Start writing, now!' You can always force yourself to get up an hour earlier in the morning or cancel your Netflix subscription because no one is going to do it for you and force you to live out your dreams, just as no one is going to lose a wink of sleep if you go an entire lifetime without publishing a single word.

But if you are ready to change your life and manifest the stories inside of you, do the one thing that will make a difference: Write. Now. Even if—especially if—the rest of the world could care less.

## Start with a Short Story

This guide to manifesting a story can take several routes. One could be the completion of a short story, a manageable task for a three-week period, though a short story's strict economy of words leaves little room for errors. Each paragraph counts, just as each word counts in a poem. If you stall in a paragraph, you may lose your reader, whereas in a novel you can afford a less-than perfect chapter or two. The advantage of short fiction, however, is that it allows you to go through the entire writing process in a minimal period of time.

If you go the route of a novella or novel, the lessons of storytelling, structure, and techniques are going to be the same overall, though your aim will be the completion of one to three chapters. In either case, sticking to a strict habit of writing for 21 days will improve your life in several ways. Among other things, it will:

- Give you as sense of accomplishment

- Discipline your mind

- Open the doors to a community of writers or artists

- Provide a new direction to your life

- Officially mark your life as a serious writer

The purpose of this book is to change your overall approach to writing. After three weeks, writing will no longer be a hobby, a pastime, or unfulfilled dream. Rather, it will be a significant part of your regimen of daily responsibilities. Whether that writing eventually turns into a money-making career or not is beyond the scope of this book. We suggest that you instead embrace the lack of external pressures as a writer. During the next few weeks, no one is going to demand you to produce something polished or publish-ready. You are not going to miss your publisher's deadline. You are not adapting your story to an agent's or editor's own preferences. Readers are not going to beat you up online with bad reviews.

So enjoy your anonymity! It is a freedom that you may not always have. During this time you can make mistakes without recourse. You can oppose literary trends and expectations and write something completely original, unique, and mystifying. Maybe someday you will need to navigate the challenges of a published and public writer. Until then, you are free to write what you want.

## Be Fearless

Writing derives its meaning from action. Writing is what you do. Writing is proactive, a way of life, one of the most important of solitary behaviors. We suggest you approach the next three weeks of your writing routine with the mindset of the Japanese hero-warrior, the Samurai. To put it simply, a Samurai's life was one of discipline, hard work, submission to one's master, and a constant surrender of one's ego until there was nothing to inhibit his training, development, and growth as a warrior. Before a Samurai finally entered the battlefield, he would envision his own death and accept its imminence, showing both courage and honor before he had even stepped onto the battlefield.

In the same way, you need to imagine that nobody will care about the story you write over the next three weeks—that no matter how well your story comes out, nothing will come of it. Assume it will be rejected by literary webzines, ignored by friends, even disliked by family members. Since literary 'death' is probable, you might as well go down swinging.

Much of the time we are so concerned with pleasing an imaginary audience that that is exactly what we get: a story that resonates with no one. You can be so concerned by what people *might* think that you end up writing a story you don't even like. That is not to say you should ignore your target audience, but that you become that target audience first and write the story you have always wanted to read. Once you have overcome this mental hurdle, you will be free from what dooms all ammature writers to mediocrity and irrelevance: fear.

Imagine yourself at your table or desk at 5AM or 10PM writing when most people are in bed warm and cozy. Your eyes droop, your back aches, your imagination stalls...and you write anyway. It all boils down to creating a consistent pattern of behavior for three weeks, which is not a ground-breaking approach. Even if you don't follow the step-by-step process of this book, at least make the time to write every day for 21 days and you will not just produce the draft of a story or the start of a novel, more importantly you will have lived as a writer enough to navigate the risk of failure and believe you will pull yourself off the cliff of each narrative obstacle that comes in your way.

## How to Use This Book

There are two ways to use this book. First of all, this is a short book, an intentional decision to focus more on writing rather than reading.

The last thing we want to do is give you another excuse not to write. So when you have read enough for one day to get your engine running, stop reading and begin writing! If you get nothing else from this book, write everyday until it becomes a habit, a behavior, and a belief in yourself. Whenever you see the subtitle 'Now Write,' it is a reminder of the one thing that needs to happen every day.

But you may need to use this book as a literal step-by-step manual because you have not mastered the writing process. If you follow the writing exercise for each day, not only will you develop your story, you will avoid making the major writing errors that mark incompetent stories.

Feel free to move through certain 'days' or even a week far more quickly than what is suggested, especially when you find increasing momentum. Every writer is different, and while outlining may require extra mental effort and time for some, it may come naturally to you and require less time. Move ahead to the next day or week if you have more time on your hands or if you get through the step quicker. Spend time on the steps and story elements your story needs the most. At the same time, don't stall. As a step-by-step manual, this is meant to keep you progressing and to eliminate writer's block.

## A Writing Resource

The other way to use this book is as a writing resource. While it is not intended to be an exhaustive resource of literary techniques, it does cover many story elements and rules of style that all writers need to master. Using this as a resource instead of a manual will be analogous to taking a class asynchronously. While your classmates will require the daily lessons to stay on track, you are going to move at your own pace and achieve the same goal. But do not take shortcuts. Write daily for 21 days straight for as much time as your life allows.

The first goal is write. The second is to write well. The rest will take care of itself.

## Illustrated Examples

Throughout this book we will refer to a variety of stories, novels, and movies as illustrations of good writing techniques. We allude to three short stories frequently because they are, firstly, great stories; secondly, you may have already read them in freshmen English; and thirdly, they are short enough for you to read in brief intervals of time. The stories are:

"The Most Dangerous Game" by Richard Connell

"The Scarlett Ibis" by James Hurst

"A Good Man is Hard to Find" by Flannery O'Conner

We also reference a story we wrote called "Regret" that was conceived for the purposes of illustrating the writing process we outline in this book. The excerpts of brainstorming, passages, dialogue, and narration were created while following the processes and activities of each day's tasks. However, a draft of the completed story is not included in this edition of the book as it would be a distraction of our purposes. (Connect with us on social media for free access to this story along with our latest advice and tips.)

# Week 1: The Brainstorm

# DAY 1

## Focus on Quality, not Length

The goal of the first three days is to conceive a strong idea for a story. Whether your idea is fit for a 6,000 word short story or a 60,000 word novel does not matter if you do not have an inspiring idea. Besides, it's far more important to write a memorable short story than a forgettable novel. (Alternately, if you are not an experienced writer, you might as well make your mistakes in the form of a short story and *then* move on.)

To put it simply, don't waste your time on a merely 'good' idea for a story. There is little difference between good and bad in the arts. 'Good' writing means nothing and is practically interchangeable with 'bad' writing. A 'good' book might be so average, so forgettable that someone thinks it's actually bad. A movie might be barely above average to the point that some will only notice its narrative failures and miss its redemptive qualities altogether.

One of the most influential and alluded to stories of suspense and survival ever written is "The Most Dangerous Game" by Richard Connell. In the short story, a world-renown hunter becomes stranded on a remote island owned by wealthy, sociopathic hunter who has run out of challenging game to hunt and is now looking for a smarter, more sophisticated prey...people. This story's concept was so intriguing it turned into multiple film and TV adaptations, while being a masterpiece in its own right despite its relatively short 11,500 word count.

The point is not to take your story idea for granted. Your creative efforts will get more mileage and enjoyment if you are spinning a tale that only takes a single sentence to inspire you (and future readers).

## Now Write:

Write a list of story ideas. These ideas should be no longer than a single sentence or fragment that describe a conflict with a sense of intrigue, mystery, or danger. Write at least a dozen ideas. Have fun with this list. Include ideas you've been kicking around for some time, but also write down fresh ideas that come to your mind and discover the gold buried deep inside.

Come up with ideas that excite your imagination that tempt you to drop everything and begin writing them. Create a list that makes it nearly impossible from which to choose, and then spend the next 24 hours mulling it through.

## EXAMPLE:

*- A man regrets his life right before dying and calls out to God for a second chance ("Regret")*

*- A boy decides to look for his dad who has abandoned his family*

*- A girl goes to school one day and realizes that she is literally invisible*

*- A dog decides that his species is uncivilized and tries to fit in with human society.*

*- A woman discovers that her husband is a serial killer as they leave the country for their 10th wedding anniversary.*

If you are desperate for a story idea, feel free to use any of the above, or take one and adjust it. None of these have been written, except the first one. Even better, see what fascinating ideas come spilling out of your mind!

## Next:

Your difficult job now is to choose three of the best ideas from your list. From our experience, the best ideas are the ones that come easy to write; its inception should be effortless by aligning with your interests, experience, instinct, and imagination. But sometimes there is no other way of knowing which idea will work out until you spend some time free-writing.

Free-write about each of these three ideas and explore where they take you. Explore who the characters are, what the character arc (change) will be, where it will take place, and what inspires you most about this story. Write about each story idea for ten to fifteen minutes straight without stopping.

# DAY 2

## Test it Out!

Even if you have fallen in love with an idea by now, you need to rephrase it in a concise way that reveals how strong it is. It should answer the following three questions with a strong affirmation:

1. Is it intriguing, mysterious, or unique?
2. Is there a character arc?
3. Does it say something important?

## EXAMPLE:

*A man experiences an epiphany about the selfish decisions he has made in his life and then spends the story tracking down all of the relationships he messed up in order to fix them.*

The above idea misses the first question outright, and the other two partially. It lacks intrigue and sounds like a generic take on Ebenezer Scrooge without the spirits in the dead of night. What is his character arc? Does he actually make amends? Doe he fail? This story could say something important, but needs more work.

Take your favorite idea and revise it until it is more focused, more important, more fascinating than any other story you've ever written. Here is a revised version of the above example:

## EXAMPLE:

*In the split second before his death rock climbing, a man named Clint realizes he has made a mess of his relationship with his ex-wife and daughter. As he clings for his life on edge of a cliff, he promises God that he will fix these relationships if he survives. Miraculously, another climber comes to his rescue out of nowhere. As the man excitedly makes plans to right these wrongs, he is haunted by the thought that he will not be able to overcome the same flaws that made his life a mess in the first place.*

This is a better synopsis because it is has the promise of mystery: Was it divine intervention that saved him? Will he be similarly punished if he doesn't fix his life? It also has a character arc, which we will discuss in length. Finally, the story will focus on the universal theme of regret and the potential for redemption.

## Now Write:

Pick one of your short story ideas and revise it until it answers all of the *Test it Out* questions.

# DAY 3

## Brainstorming

Brainstorming removes the dam of the conscious and orderly mind, allowing your imagination to flow without the impediment of rules, conventions, or standards. Our brains are wired to turn chaos into order, but sometimes we need to let out some of the creative chaos lurking in our subconscious, allow the hurricane of an idea to hit our keyboard until it breaks into a hundred tornadoes in a hundred directions. Only more time on the keyboard, more time running through the terrain of our logic, will a single story finally settle into place. To use a different analogy, brainstorming is not so much throwing everything at a wall and seeing what sticks; it is chiseling away at different stones to discover the statues hidden in them. The more you write, the more your imagination chisels away...the more beauty you bring out of *the formless*.

Though it is tempting to think that you are done conceptualizing your story after a brief amount of free writing, its depth and potential can only be unlocked by something as open-form and investigative as the brainstorming process. Many inexperienced writers take an idea and begin the drafting process too early, assuming that what comes out is a rough draft when it is really a glorified manuscript of more brainstorming—a sloppy and in-cohesive mess. Get the messiness out of you in the next week. Play in the sandbox of your imagination and let it go wild. There are no rules, no boundaries, no criteria for brainstorming other than giving yourself the time and freedom to explore the full potential of your story idea.

At some point you need to get out of the sandbox and get down to the work of outlining, but we suggest you return to the task of brainstorming anytime you hit a dead-end in the writing process.

## Now Write:

Thoroughly brainstorm your story idea. Let your mind race and follow where it goes. Brainstorm the personal history of each character. Describe your settings and the kind of mood you want your story to have. Keep in mind, this is just the first of several brainstorming sessions, so don't rush it or put too much pressure on yourself. Feel free to draw, diagram, use verse, write full scenes of dialogue, describe your setting, and dig into your story's themes.

## Extra challenge:

Write down a random physical object and setting, both interesting and unconnected to your story. Don't overthink this. Literally write down the first things that come to your mind!

As you brainstorm, figure out how to weave this random item and setting into your story. Whether they provide a connection between plot points or simply provide texture to your story, the purpose is to stretch your imagination as you write and include possibilities you might not otherwise have considered.

# Day 4

This day has two writing activities: creating a title and a character arc. If you already have a title for your story, skip right to the character arc. If you have *not* spent time thinking about your title, do so now; however, the title to your story can also wait for that perfect phrase that emerges organically in the midst of your narration.

## The Right Title

Sometimes the title of a story comes as quickly and easily as the idea. A story idea might even begin with a title that pops into your head and you build your story around it. Other times, a title becomes your way of grabbing your readers' attention. Think about "The Hunger Games," which arouses an irresistible curiosity. What kind of society would turn the misery of hunger into a sport? Or a title can be the key to a story's theme and meaning. James Hurst's short story "The Scarlet Ibis" references an exotic bird whose fragility represents human weakness and its color violence. A title can also be ironic and throw your readers for a loop. Flannery O'Conner's classic short story "A Good Man is Hard to Find" is not about a woman's long list of failed relationships, but an elderly woman's fateful encounter with a cold-blooded killer who challengers her view of humanity. And who wouldn't want to read a story called "The Most Dangerous Game"?

At the risk of sounding obvious, be sure that your title actually sounds good. Once in a while you will see the titles of stories, books, TV shows, or movies that have no ring to them. Like poetry, a title needs to have some rhythm to it and evoke mystery or emotion.

In our example story, we chose a simple title, "Regret." Whether this is a great title or not, we can not objectively judge, but regret is a universal emotion and has a nice muted sound to it. The word is somber, hinting at loss and missed opportunities. It also foreshadows the story's ending.

The beauty of choosing a title now is that it can help you focus your story. Think of your story title as a promise to your reader. Just as a reader judges a book by its cover—fairly or unfairly—the cover is judged largely by the title that appears on it.

## The Protagonist's Character Arc

The success of your entire story depends on the interaction of two story elements: your protagonist and his/her story arc. Nothing else matters in your story compared to these. You can have beautiful prose, a fascinating idea, an immersive world, and gut-wrenching drama, but if nobody cares about your protagonist—or your character has nowhere to go in terms of growth or change—your readers are likely to lose interest. If your protagonist is just window dressing for your plot (even if the genre in which you are writing is plot heavy) your readers might go shopping elsewhere. Your protagonist is the reason your reader is going to care about your plot in the first place.

A character arc is the story of a character's *change* from the beginning of the story to the end. This change should be extreme—as in a homebound Hobbit taking on devilish orcs—making the arc satisfying. But how should a character arc work? Follow these two rules:

1. Make the arc (the course of change) extremely difficult—requiring much pain, training, battles, and important lessons along the way.
2. Keep the arc simple. Don't make the mistake of making the arc too easy or, alternately, too convoluted.

Your protagonist's life should be a mess at the beginning of the story, if not a complete disaster—more Jimmy Stewart than John Wayne. The growth should be fairly linear as well. Each challenge, battle, and painful experience along the way needs to add to his/her growth, increasing his/her capacity to rise up to the challenge at the end—an otherwise impossible feat save for the growth along the way.

In our example story "Regret," Clint's ideal character arc *should* take him from a state of selfishness and regret to a life of responsibility and self-control, except that he does not change enough to see this arc through, dying before he is given another chance to follow through with his promises.

## The Antagonist

The antagonist is not just a 'bad guy,' but the source of conflict and other any force acting against the protagonist. There are two rules to follow when creating your antagonist, whether it is a person or an inner flaw. Antagonists should be:

1. An unstoppable force
2. Beautifully complex

Whether human or not, an antagonist should be highly motivated and pose great danger. Whether it is the Joker, Thanos, or Anton Chigurh from "No Country For Old Men," an antagonist is the hero of his/her own story, having overcome great challenges and proven to be worthy of any opponent. Not just anyone is going to stop them. For one, strong antagonists have an unquenchable desire to accomplish their goals, driven by passion and perseverance. If you don't understand your antagonist's goals and motivation, you need to brainstorm until you do.

Secondly, villains should be courageous to the point of over-confidence, which is the reason people are attracted to villains in stories. They embody unusual confidence and courage, approaching each obstacle that gets in their way with swagger—the kind of confidence that a hero does not possess at the beginning of the story, and the kind of vanity that will always separate villains from heroes. Make your villains confident, courageous, and thoroughly motivated.

Use the same approach if your story's central conflict is an internal one. If your protagonist's internal antagonist is excessive pride (hubris), show how it leads to self-destruction. In "Regret," Clint's capacity for self-absorption and vanity doesn't just deprive him of a meaningful relationship with his daughter; it puts her and her mother in mortal danger at the end of the story...while sending him literally over a cliff. With either type of antagonist (internal or external) your protagonist should feel completely outmatched at the beginning of the story. His/her only hope is growing stronger with each battle along the way.

The second rule you must follow with antagonists is to make them beautifully complex. By creating a such a paradox—an ugly force with sympathetic humanity—you will tap into the most universal of themes: the tragic downfall of potentially great people. Children don't grow up hoping to be criminals one day. Even the worst of humanity started off as innocent boys or girls needing to be loved by their mothers and fathers, and many criminals (if not most?) view themselves as misunderstood victims themselves. If your antagonist is a person, make him/her motivated by fundamental emotions and just as sympathetic and human as your protagonist, wrenching your readers' emotions in multiple directions. What makes "The Godfather" so gut wrenching and sublime is the depiction of the mob family's criminal patriarch as empathetic as it is sociopathic.

For an internal conflict, show the root of your protagonist's 'inner demons' that are causing mayhem, but also avoid the mistake of oversimplification. An alcoholic's life doesn't change overnight just because he/she joins an AA program. Depression should not be illustrated in broad strokes with a simple solution. A poor self-image doesn't improve because of a new relationship. Take our protagonist Clint for example: He loves his daughter and sincerely wants to turn his life around. But in the end he wants the results of a 'good' life more than he wants the sacrifices of a 'good' life. Our goal is to show how sincere he is about wanting change and his internal resistance to that change.

In a story with primarily internal antagonists (in the form of inner flaws) turn at least one of your supporting characters into an unwitting/unintentional antagonist. In "Regret," Clint meets a beautiful named Sheila who might have been a good match, except that their timing is wrong and her penchant for risk-taking distracts Clint from his mission of self-improvement, unintentionally sabotaging attempt to salvage his relationship with his daughter. Sheila serves as a foil for Clint's current state of mind (we discuss *foil* in the next chapter). By fawning on his looks and indulging his love of weekend getaways and drinking, she takes him farther from his path of redemption. She is not intentionally 'antagonizing' his growth, but is far more motivated in her contradictory life goals than he is.

To make your story more interesting and complex, consider creating secondary characters who complicate the protagonist's growth without being the stereotypical 'bad guy.'

## Now Write:

1. Write a list of working titles. Search the internet for your favorite title to be sure it is not overused, or used in your same genre. This does not mean it has to be totally original. A cooking book titled "Baker's Dozen" can co-exist in a library with a serial-killer story about a murderous cook.

2. Brainstorm your protagonist's character arc. Discuss his/her shortfalls and flaws, along with a worthy antagonist who is fearless, determined, and complex.

# DAY 5

## Supporting Characters

We could go over an exhaustive list of archetypical characters, but as you plow through the first draft of this story and establish your new writing routine, you only need to be aware of two critical roles for supporting characters:

1) They help characterize your protagonist.

2) They support your protagonist in his/her journey.

We are not going to lose sight of the overall goal of this book: to encourage you to behave like a writer daily until you believe you are one. You can leave it to critics to overanalyze the characters in your story as fitting certain archetypal categories, but all you need to understand is that secondary characters matter only as much as they support your protagonist and provide a stark contrast.

## Foils

To bring out your protagonist's personality, use a supporting character's personality as a foil (complete contrast). If your protagonist is cerebral and quiet, his/her friend should be outspoken and chatty, or vice versa. Whoever surrounds your protagonist—whether friends, allies, rivals, or comedic relief—should display contrasting characteristics to help paint a more vivid picture of your protagonist.

A more advanced technique is using a supporting character to gauge how much your protagonist changes from the beginning to the end of an arc. In "The Most Dangerous Game" the protagonist Rainsford is traveling down a jungle river with a hunting crew on the hunt for jaguars. Rainsford's hunting partner is a compassionate man named

Whitney who shares his sympathy for the jaguars they hunt. Rainsford laughs off this theory, suggesting prey have no capacity for fear. Whitney's empathetic views sets the stage, not just for Rainsford's soon-to-be precarious situation in a madman's game, but to also contrast his growth by the end of the story when he knows exactly how it feels to be hunted.

In "The Scarlet Ibis," Doodle is a handicapped boy whose compassion for all living things is contrasted sharply with his able-bodied brother's inability to show empathy. This contrast is the source of the narrator's inner conflict, and is only possible because the younger brother is a foil physically, emotionally, and motivationally to the narrator.

## Guides

If a protagonist's struggle is truly heroic—or at least beyond the capacity of their early state—it should require the help of others. Archetypical help often comes in the form of a mentor, guide, or mother figure, but it can be any character who pushes the protagonist to exceed his/her current level of development. Your supporting characters who guide or help a protagonist's challenge should, simultaneously, be an antagonist in their own way—a force of resistance to a hero's inner flaws—provoking them to growth.

In "Regret," Clint's daughter and ex-wife pressure him to be responsible and follow through with his commitments. As long as he is helping his ex-wife or spending time with his daughter, he is living up to his potential and turning his life around. In this story, however, there will be no guide or mentor to help Clint see the error of his ways when he begins to stray, which is one reason he is not able to overcome his fatal flaw.

# Other Advice about Supporting Characters

- Whatever you do, don't allow supporting characters to steal the spotlight from the protagonist. If you have done your job coming up with a compelling main character, no other character matters outside of his/her journey. Supporting characters serve to help illustrate the protagonist's journey from Point A—not being able to overcome the obstacles in the way—to Point B—the moment he/she finally can. That is it.

- Limit the number of supporting characters! Again, apart from the protagonist's journey, they don't matter, so there is no reason to be gratuitous in cluttering your story with unnecessary characters to keep track of.

- Know your characters inside out. You should know the food they like, the books they read, the physical ailments that afflict them. You should know how they talk: the slang they use, the extent of their education and vocabulary, the part of the country from which they originate, the dialect they use, etc. Your characters need to sound like individuals, not stock caricatures pulled out of a cereal box.

- Finally, be intentional about naming your characters, whether their names symbolize their attributes—think of Samwise Gamgee (who is wise), Han Solo (who depends on no one), and President Snow (cold and pure in his ambition)—or simply represent their invented ancestry. Whatever you do, avoid the mistake of giving your characters names that sound similar to each other. One of the biggest rookie mistakes that leaps off the page immediately is when characters feel interchangeable—their names and personalities blend together without distinction.

## Now Write:

Write your short list of characters and brainstorm about them. Who is the foil, the guide, the help? Write about their past, their personalities, even their ancestry. Write about their strengths and weaknesses, their secrets and dreams, and most importantly how they contrast with your protagonist in significant ways. Write about what worries them and gives them purpose. Brainstorm about their likes and dislikes, the way they speak, including pet phrases. Finally, brainstorm their names, being intentional about how they sound and what they mean.

# DAY 6

## A Killer Climax

In order to guarantee that your story will make an impact, go to the very end of your story and imagine the climax, the moment of truth, the most consequential fight your protagonist must face. Push your protagonist to the brink. In the second week of this process, you will outline the climax in greater detail, but the goal now is to imagine a harrowing scene of great consequence, pitting your protagonist against the antagonist in a way that would have meant certain defeat at the beginning of the story. Think of the worst case scenario that your antagonist could possibly present. Only then will you know what your protagonist must endure, learn, and survive in order to meet this final challenge.

Nothing is worse in modern action films than when protagonists ("John Wick," "Rebel Moon," anything with Jason Statham) do not earn their ability to defeat opponents effortlessly. At least Daniel LaRusso in "The Karate Kid" (Ralph Macchio version) was humiliated by bullies and had to spend hours doing muscle-building chores before he could pull off one good kick by the end of the movie. Brainstorming a climax now allows you to reverse engineer the rest of the plot.

How will you know if your climactic scene is good enough? For one, it should be impossible for your protagonist to handle if it takes place earlier in the story. Secondly, it should contrast in every way to the beginning of the story. Whereas the ending shows your protagonist taking on monumental challenges head-on, they should be reticent in the beginning. The world should be full of a gray in the beginning, whereas everything turns to black and white by the end.

The climax should also define the middle of your story because there needs to be a moment of crisis and defeat that foreshadows the final showdown, exposing the protagonist's growth and vulnerability—a 'cocoon' moment where instead of 'dying' the protagonist grows in capacity to develop into the hero they will eventually become. Basically, the potential of your entire story resides on how dangerous, how challenging, how impossible the climactic moment of your story is…determining the extent of your protagonist's arc.

Two classic examples of short stories with killer climaxes are "The Scarlet Ibis" and "A Good Man is Hard to Find" by Flannery O'Connor. "The Scarlett Ibis" is a Cain and Abel story of an older brother who must constantly look out for his disabled younger brother. At the climax of the story, the narrator abandons his sickly younger brother, Doodle, in a thunderstorm, attempting to outrun his caretaking responsibilities. We hear Doodle's weak voice cry out for help in the midst of a storm, his weak heart giving out to the narrator's horror. In "A Good Man is Hard to Find," a grandmother is confronted by a killer while her family is dragged off to the woods to be shot. The grandmother engages her killer with philosophical and religious questions as shots ring out from the woods. These climactic moments are disturbing and impossible to set down and are the catalysts for the completion of the main characters' arc: without tragic consequences, neither protagonist would have changed by the end of their stories.

Below is our brainstorming of the climactic ending of "Regret":

*Though I am not sure exactly of all the reasons that have led to this moment, Clint has been invited by a beautiful woman named Sheila to hike at a local mountain range. She knows he loves to climb and hike. She tells him it is not a technically difficult hike, except one part, which is dangerous and he needs to be sure to have good shoes. The date of this hike conflicts with a commitment he's already made with his ex-wife and daughter.*

*The reader knows that this hiking date will most likely lead to his death because Clint barely survived the last time he was on a mountain, and he has not taken advantage of his second chance to make things right in his life. When he comes up with excuses about why he can't help his ex-wife move out of her apartment that weekend—something she needs help with, which would also give him a chance to hang out with his daughter AND protect them from being harassed by the stalker in the apartment from whom his wife is trying to get away—readers will not sympathize with his own consequences. Rather, the reader will almost hope he falls off a cliff this time and that he finally learns his lesson before he dies.*

*Things come to a head as he and Sheila reach the dangerous part of the hike. We flash to his ex-wife back at the apartment as the stalker attempts to break into her apartment, their daughter locking herself in the bathroom. Back at the mountain, Clint loses his footing and begins to slide off the cliff and attempts to catch himself before plunging off it. The reader at this point has such little compassion for Clint and is only left wondering what his last thoughts will be and whether he is going to cry out to God again or will he finally realize how he can't blame anyone but himself for the terrible person he has been all these years right up to the last moment.*

This brainstorming rambles a bit, but it paints a rough picture of where the story needs to go. Instead of just having Clint shrug off his promise to be with his daughter and help her and her mom move out that weekend, we increased the stakes by including the character of the stalker. We don't know if the stalker idea is too convoluted, but it magnifies the consequences of his selfish decisions.

## A Lasting Image

"The Scarlet Ibis" ends with the unsettling image of the older brother cradling Doodle—beautiful in his heart and frail in his body, a scarlet stain of blood on his mouth. The description of the dying boy is vivid and sharp, as is the older brother's emotional response. The theme of the story is expressed so clearly in this final description that there is no confusion about its meaning and no less powerful in its brevity.

In "A Good Man is Hard to Find," the grandmother, who is about to be shot and killed by the 'Misfit,' has a vision of Heaven before dying. This vision is a picture of an inclusive heaven that destroys her life-long prejudice of humanity. The final images in both stories are vivid, difficult to read, and make you think a long time after you are finished reading. As you continue to brainstorm, ask yourself what is that stark, lasting image with which you want your story to end? If describing this scene does not make your heart race, your eyes tear, or blood boil, then it is not good enough.

In "Regret," Clint's last moments on the cliff will provide the opportunity to say something important about living a life of selfishness. It will end with Clint's feeling of regret—not just about his decisions in life—but lying to himself about all the excuses he made along the way.

## Give it a Twist

If you are writing a short story, there is no better form to use to pull the rug out from under your reader so effectively. Novels with a big plot twist can sometimes feel like a betrayal—as if all of the expectations that the writer has created were only created as manipulation to trick the reader. Personally, we have no stomach for stories in any medium that reveal that the entire story was just a dream at the end. Such a twist, especially in a novel or a movie, can feel insincere, especially when the reader has invested so much time and emotion in something they assumed was 'real.' Besides, this has been effectively two or three times in literature, and that's enough ("The Wizard of Oz," Tim O'Brien's "The Things They Carried," Ian McEwan's "Atonement") and writers just need to move on to more inventive twists.

In a short story, a reader actually hopes to be amazed, shocked, or moved in a few pages of reading, much like seeing a magician use slight of hand to simulate magic, so it is the perfect medium to shake up your reader's expectations. In addition, the beginning of the story will be so fresh in the reader's mind that the twist will hit in the right way, allowing you to overdeliver on whatever simple premise upon which your story is based. If you are writing a novel, your twist needs to braided throughout your story and thus requires a lot of planning and brainstorming so that it is more than just a parlor trick.

## Now Write:

Brainstorm the climax of your story. Describe how you will make an impact, what the imagery that is is going to communicate this impact, and explore possible ways to use misdirection along the way. But don't create a twist for the sake of shock value. The ending needs to fit the overall tone and theme of your story.

From there, begin reverse-engineering the rest of your story, including the middle that should be a dress rehearsal of your protagonist's final test because you need a moment to reveal his/her vulnerability—if not failure—to force the protagonist to grow.

# DAY 7

## Thematic Statement

Have you yet considered what your story means or why it matters? What does it say about life, the world, or relationships? The answer to these questions is, of course, your secret alone...and should probably stay that way. Writers typically avoid answering questions about their story's meaning so as not to rob a reader's own interpretation, allowing the story to become the reader's own personal experience. So why should you be concerned about the theme?

Because you need every element in your story—both in plot and idea—to align. Your story's underlying meaning must be consistent with its character arc, plot structure, and resolution. Minimally, its theme should not be contradictory. Story elements are, after all, a codex of images for your story's meaning. There doesn't have to be a single interpretation of your story, and the only key to cracking your story's code should be its symmetry. It is not your job to tell the reader what your story means, only to make sure the explicit or implicit theme lines up with everything else.

What if you just want to tell a genre story? Don't let genre limit its depth. Just because you write a romance, suspense, thriller, or fantasy doesn't mean it should say nothing about the human condition. Rather, the founding writers of genre—whether it was Poe creating the horror genre, Tolkien creating fantasy, or Mary Shelley shaping gothic—used plot, setting, and mood in new ways to bring a haunting perspective of the human condition.

## Now Write:

Write your thematic statement to guarantee there is a thought structure to your story. Be sure to not reference your character's names or the events of the story. Again, this is your secret, a magician's secret, that you will reveal to no one.

## EXAMPLE:

*We sacrifice long-term relationships for short-term gratification, and most of us would repeat these same mistakes even if given a second chance to avoid disaster.*

# Wrap up of Week 1

In the first seven days, the goal is to have a killer story idea (not necessarily about murder) with a strong vision of structure, fully realized characters, a powerful ending, and a theme underpinning it all. Spend as much time brainstorming these ideas during this first week. None of it will go to waste because your exploration will lead to discoveries you would not otherwise make.

## Product of Week 1

- Pages of notes (written or typed)

- Long passages of brainstorming that sketch out your protagonist

- A clear vision of your character arc

- Character sketches of your supporting characters and their roles in the story, including backgrounds, personalities, and contrasts

- Rough outlining of how your story leads to its climax

- Samples of dialogue between the characters in dramatic or important moments.

# Week 2: The Outline

## The Main Conflict and Complications

Once you have a strong vision of this story, it is time to write an official outline. Some of you will fright at the thought of anything resembling an outline. That is okay. 'Pantsers' enjoy writing by the 'seat of their pants' and derive a good deal of their creative energy from problem-solving their own mysteries, while 'outliners' need to be reassured of the integrity of their story's structure by outlining everything. Either way, a story needs a tight structure and a freshness throughout. That means you need a defined skeleton of a plot that moves naturally from one event to the next until arriving at the only place it could have from the start—the climactic scene that defines your story.

The sole purpose of the outline is to keep the story focused and to put the essential parts—the conflict, protagonist, setting, character arc, and theme—in their proper places without getting in the way of each other. Good structure does not bring attention to its scaffolded plot devices and character types.

To avoid bringing attention to the fact that you designed each part of your story for a particular effect, do not spend too much time on any one part. For example, the beginning of your outline should be only long enough to introduce your protagonist, setting, and inciting incident, and then move on. If you linger, the reader is pulled out of the story and wonders when you are going to 'get on' with the story, so be strategic with your outline to accomplish two goals:

1. Deepen the main conflict of your protagonist with complications.

1.  Keep your reader wondering what will happen next.

If you divert from the main conflict, your story will lose steam and emotional power. Alternately, if you do not continue to complicate the story with suspense, your reader may become bored or lose interest. Plotting is a paradoxical endeavor—the need to focus on one thing (main conflict) and then to complicate that one thing. But imagine "A Christmas Carol" with only one ghost. Each additional ghost peels away another dimension of Scrooge's character, providing a more complex portrait of his life, raising the stakes of his current path of doom. The more complications, the greater a character arc, and the more powerful the story. Like a river cutting a path to the ocean, the main conflict drives the protagonist's story arc while the complications feed it like streams, increasing the strength and energy as the story moves forward towards the climax.

The brainstorming/free-writing process is informal work done in a robe and slippers while downing cup after cup of coffee in a mad frenzy as the ideas pour out of your head. The outlining process, on the other hand, is where you put on work clothes, sit at a desk, and get down to the business of drawing out your story's blueprints. Each part of the outline needs to be intrinsically entertaining and meaningful on its own, while simultaneously flowing to the next part and engineered to have, by story's end, a singular effect and meaning.

# DAY 8

## The Opening Scene

Plan out the opening scene in detail, which needs to be compelling as it introduces the main characters (not too many!), the setting, a conflict, and a compelling reason to read, all within the first page. This is a short work of fiction. There's no time to world-build or play in the sand. Get right down to business! That is not to say jump straight into an action sequence because you don't want overwhelm your reader. But do all of the above in a way that simultaneously introduces your protagonist's current (unacceptable) state of being and the situation that leads to your inciting incident.

## EXAMPLE outline of "Regret"

    *A.  Opening Scene*

        *1.  A man named Clint is climbing solo on a mountain when he loses his grip and begins to slide off the cliff.*

        *2.  As he is about to die, he realizes his life has been a waste, that he has failed his daughter and ex-wife.*

        *3.  Just before he lets go, Clint calls out to God to save him. He promises to change his selfish ways, to become a better father to his daughter, and make things right with his ex-wife.*

## Now Write:

Outline your opening scene. Introduce your setting and protagonist while setting up your inciting incident. Summarize each major detail in no more than one to three sentences.

# DAY 9

## The Inciting Incident

If the opening scene is the bait, the inciting incident is the hook that catches your reader. The inciting incident follows the opening scene and *introduces your conflict and antagonist*, the exact moment your plot kicks into gear and where your protagonist is set on a specific journey to restore order to the world or his/her own inner being. Whether you have an actual antagonist or not, there needs to be a moment where the world has been turned upside down for your protagonist—a moment of no return. In a hero's tale, something has forced the hero to come out of the comfort of his/her own home. The evil will not stay at bay, and the hero is no longer going to stand by and become its victim.

## EXAMPLE Outline of "Regret"

    A. *Inciting Incident*
        1. *Another climber comes out of nowhere and saves Clint right before he falls. The climber pulls Clint to safety and gives him water.*
        2. *After Clint catches his breath, he tries thanking the climber, but the mysterious climber is nowhere to be seen.*
        3. *Clint assumes this was divine intervention, but whether or not it was an angel or a man, Clint knows he needs to follow through with his promise to himself and to God.*
        4. *When he leaves the mountain and returns home, Clint is confronted with the question of whether he is in fact capable of avoiding the same selfish mistakes that made a mess of his life in the first place.*

> 5. *Clint creates a list of things he will do to rectify his wrongs. At the end of this list he writes, "I will surely fail because I am not the man who can do all of these things. That is why I need to change. But will I?"*

In the above example, the inciting incident involves Clint's promise to change his life and fix his relationship with his daughter and ex-wife while confronting the ultimate question of whether he has the will-power to do so. He knows he cannot. He knows he needs to change in order to follow through with his list of good deeds. With his antagonistic traits of self-doubt and weakness now introduced, the gears of the plot have been put into motion.

## Now Write:

Outline your inciting incident, writing one to three sentences per detail. Be sure to introduce your antagonist and main conflict, both internal and external.

Here are other questions to consider for the inciting incident:

- Does the end of your story depend up on what happens in your inciting incident?

- Has the proverbial line been drawn in the sand from this moment forward?

- Has your protagonist's life been changed forever?

- Has your protagonist's world shrunk down to a single event?

# DAY 10

## Introducing Complications

One of your jobs as an author is rather sadistic: to make your protagonist's life as miserable as possible. Ironically, the more miserable you make your protagonist's life, the greater your reader's catharsis. Catharsis is the release of pent up emotions—being brought to tears when a protagonist's own misery has reached a breaking point. Stories can move us deeply because we invest time and vicarious sympathy in the fictional character's struggles, triggering our own repressed pain. We spend so much energy keeping our unprocessed or unhealed pain locked up inside just to survive the day that when we let our emotional guard down for a story, movie, song, play, or piece of art, our wound-up emotional ball of yarn can easily begin to unwind.

Whether or not you trigger catharsis in your reader is not really something you can control or should worry about. What you can control, however, is making your protagonist's life as complicated and painful as possible. The main conflict should quickly spiral into multiple related conflicts that worsen as the story unfolds until the moment where the protagonist and antagonist can no longer coexist and one must overcome the other.

These complications should not be random obstacles, nor should they be predictable. They should be precise in their effect, strong in their imagery, exact in their meaning, natural in their pacing, and constantly make the reader wonder, 'What is going to happen next?' Your plotting should proceed more like poetry rather than a step-by-step path from point A to point B. Depend upon your own creative instincts to find this rhythm and pacing in your outline.

Don't allow the events to feel like they have been outlined, which is admittedly paradoxical, as we've already discussed. The best story feels natural, immersive, and real. The outline can doom your story if you write it like an essay controlled by a thesis statement. Rather, the structure and meaning of your story should result from your protagonist's desperate fight against antagonizing forces. The key is figuring out how each complication naturally leads to a worse complication that simultaneously deepens the central conflict.

## EXAMPLE Outline of "Regret"

    *A.  Complications*

        *1.  Clint reviews his list of things to fix his past mistakes with his family:*

            *A.  Self-improvement: cut back his drinking, see a counselor, and be less selfish.*

            *B.  Daughter's list: schedule special outings each month, starting with the park and the circus. Take turns with his ex-wife picking up his daughter from school.*

            *C.  Ex-wife's list: start helping her move out of her apartment; confront the man at the apartment complex who has been stalking her and endangering his daughter as well. Write her an apology note.*

        *2.  Clint has a good day doing the right thing and following through with his promises: He picks up his daughter from school, takes her to the park, and returns her to her mother with whom he has a civil conversation.*

        *3.  He asks his wife about her timeline for moving out and if the stalker is bothering her. She says the stalker has not been around for some reason, which is good since she needs two weeks to move out. She asks Clint to watch their daughter the following weekend so that she look for a new apartment. He agrees.*

4. *That same week as Clint is basking in his self-approval, he meets a beautiful woman named Sheila at a cafe and talks to her for two hours straight and asks her on a date the following weekend. Consequently, Clint calls his ex-wife and cancels his plans to watch his daughter. Instead, he promises to help her move out of her apartment the following weekend.*

5. *Throughout the week, Clint discovers that Sheila knows his ex-wife from work. Sheila tells him how 'her friend from work' is moving out of her apartment because she is being stalked by someone in another apartment and her lousy ex-husband refuses to help her out. When Clint probes, he realizes that Sheila doesn't know his wife well...yet.*

6. *Sheila turns out to be a very adventurous, free-spirit who needs adventure and alcohol to be happy.*

7. *To avoid discovery or suspicion, Clint spends more and more time with Sheila and cancels all of his plans with his daughter and ex-wife, and as a result, no one confronts his ex-wife's stalker.*

## Now Write:

If you haven't figured out how your main conflict devolves into multiple complications, take the time to brainstorm now and then summarize each complication in one to three sentences in your outline.

## Extra Challenge:

If you have a strong symbol for your story, it can tie the beginning, middle, and end of your story together, while providing the kind of strong imagery a story needs. Put your symbol at the beginning of your outline, even if it feels like a random part of the setting. Then find a way to weave it into the middle of the outline, catching the attention of your protagonist during a challenging complication. Finally, insert this symbol as one of the last images you describe at the end of the story.

If I were to do this with "Regret," I could have Clint's daughter show him an angel figurine that her mother had recently bought her at a garage sale. I could have the daughter forget this angel at his house where he chooses to set it on his kitchen window. And at the end of the story I could have him grab it to take with him on his last hike as if it might provide some protection, his soul stirred by his selfish choices and fearing divine retribution. Perhaps the figurine falls out of his pocket on the hike and shatters, symbolizing the state of his soul and foreshadowing his demise.

# Day 11

## Setting up the Climax

You have already brainstormed the climax of your story, but now is the time to get serious and revise it until it is perfectly tuned. To review, whatever happens in the climax of your story needs to feel inevitable. Your protagonist is on the brink of disaster. If there was a chance to turn back, it is long gone. It is the moment where the protagonist's character is defined, where life and death hang in the balance.

Your job setting up the climax is taking away all other escape routes when the defining moment shows up. If there was a way for your protagonist to put off saving the world another day, your job is to take away that opportunity now. If you protagonist could delay facing his/her inner demon one more moment, now is the time to eliminate those excuses.

In a romantic comedy, the formula goes like this: boy meets girl, boy loses girl, boy gets girl back. What sets up a good ending to a romantic comedy is when the boy loses the girl and the outcome of the story is suddenly cast into hopelessness. In an action/adventure story, the hero is usually a social misfit who proves to be the only one qualified and courageous enough to take on a world threat. But before the final showdown, the hero suffers a defeat and setback that casts doubt on the entire mission. Your protagonist must experience something that not only foreshadows the climactic showdown to come, but illustrates the hero's mortal limitations, creating true suspense.

Because the stakes are so big at the end of a story, your greatest temptation is going to make the 'impossible' climax implausible. We will discuss plausibility at length in week three; however, ensure that everything that happens in the climax, including your protagonist's ability to survive or overcome the antagonist, is not only plausible (reasonable) but is the natural result of his/her character growth.

Your protagonist's ability to overcome his/her antagonist in the climax should be the result of whatever skills, strength, or wisdom he/she has learned as result of overcoming all of the other complications along the way. If your protagonist is going to vanquish a dragon at the end of your story with the ability to sense its weakness, then he/she should have already been thrown into a dragon's lair and learned of such weaknesses.

Don't expect your readers to accept new skills to surface at the end of story just so that he/she survives. If you need to further develop your protagonist's skillset in order to survive the climactic showdown with the antagonist, then do so now in your outline. In "Regret," Clint does not possess the internal ability to ultimately overcome his final temptation, but we don't want the ending to feel completely inevitable or predictable, so we must show that Clint has both the opportunity and the ability to change, while creating a sense of dread that he may not.

## EXAMPLE Outline of "Regret"

*D. Setting up the Climax*

1. *Clint finally follows through with one of his list items, which is to see a counselor. The counselor warns Clint about committing too quickly to this relationship with Sheila who indulges his bad habits. Rather, the counselor advises that he spend time with his daughter and follow through with his responsibilities.*

1. *Sheila invites Clint to go hiking with her at a local mountain. Clint declines and says he needs to spend time with his daughter. This upsets Sheila.*

2. *Clint learns that his ex-wife is staying with her parents because the stalker is always waiting for her at the apartment, but she still needs to move the rest of her things out. He says he will be there to help (and protect )her.*

3. *Sheila calls him one night when she is drunk and makes him feel guilty. Clint wonders if he will lose this relationship like he has all the others.*

## Now Write

Outline a scene that both foreshadows your climax and exposes your protagonist's vulnerabilities. This should include the darkest and most bleak part of the story. If your hero needs to learn a critical skill or lesson to navigate the climax, this is the time.

# DAY 12

## Outlining the Climax

If you have truly brought your protagonist to the brink of disaster, then imagine a climactic scene that is so breathtaking, so riveting, and so unlikely for your protagonist to overcome that your reader has no choice but to read through to the conclusion of your story.

And by 'unlikely,' we mean unlikely without the kind of courage, tenacity, and wisdom the protagonist has gained/discovered by overcoming prior obstacles. You must create a climax that requires not just the protagonist's employment of skills and wisdom, but the epiphany of how to use his/her skills and wisdom situationally.

Though the protagonist has changed, he/she has not lived a life of wisdom and courage long enough to become second nature. Thus, even arriving at the climax, a duality of identity exists in the protagonist. Think of Frodo at the end of the "Lord of the Rings" trilogy. While no other character has endured the burden by the end of the story without succumbing to its temptation—he has not completely mastered his self-control over the ring, putting the final outcome of the climax up in the air, pitting his courage/strength against his burden/pain.

The final test in the climax will likely drum up the protagonist's natural sense of fear and self-doubt—the feelings that have been plaguing him/her from the beginning of the story. The climax exposes this vulnerability—reminding us that the protagonist is capable of failure—before his/her strength and wisdom finally materializes at the most critical time.

So, yes, your climax needs to feel unlikely...if not for the exact experiences and lessons in the lead up to this moment.

## EXAMPLE Outline of "Regret"

*E. Climax*

1. *Shelia shows up to Clint's apartment on Saturday morning and says that she is not taking 'no' for an answer for the hike, unless he wants to break up with her at that moment. Clint doesn't want to lose Sheila and agrees to go.*
2. *She tells him to wear good shoes because there are dangerous sections of the hike (foreshadowing).*
3. *Clint calls his ex-wife to say he can't help her move out and says not to worry about the 'stalker.' He tells her she is just being paranoid.*
4. *Back at the apartment, the stalker insists on helping Clint's ex-wife move out her furniture. She accepts his help because she fears what he will do if she says no.*
5. *On the mountain hike, Clint briefly wonders how his wife and daughter are doing, feels regret for disappointing them, then tells himself he will make it up to both of them after this hike.*
6. *Inside the apartment, the stalker closes the apartment door, trapping Clint's ex-wife and daughter inside. He tells her that he has been waiting for this moment for a long time. She yells at her daughter to lock herself in the bedroom and tries calling 911. The stalker takes her phone.*
7. *Back at the mountain, Sheila stops at the edge of a cliff and asks Clint to take a selfie with her. Clint hesitates. Sheila dares him. How can he resist?*
8. *While taking the breathtaking selfie, Clint slips, begins to fall, unable to grip Sheila's outstretched hand.*

## Now Write:

Review your brainstorming for your climax. Does it still flow with the rest of your outline at this point? Does your protagonist already possess the right wisdom and skills to overcome the final challenge? Or have you set up a climax that will portray a deeper meaning if the story ends in tragedy? Do you need make adjustments based on other plot and character decisions you have made? Brainstorm until your climax is the perfect manifestation of your character's growth. Then outline accordingly.

# DAY 13

## Outlining the Resolution

Review your notes for the final image of your story. If you don't have a symbol that ties everything together, then be sure that the final image resolves your story in a way that lines up with the beginning, middle, and end of your story. The final image should remind us of how far the character has come, or should have come, since the beginning. The resolution should represent the meaning of the struggles along the way and answer the ultimate question, "Why?" If your is reader left wondering what the point of your story is at the end, it is usually the result of an incomplete or poorly planned resolution.

The ending of "Regret" is both predictable and meaningful: the reader understands that Clint's death is inevitable since he chose to abandon the people who were relying on him, illustrating the point about how we sometimes fail to take advantage of second chances and choose regret over personal sacrifice.

Do you have a symbol that you have been able to weave throughout your story? Going back to "The Scarlet Ibis," the dead bird is both fragile and beautiful and represents Doodle's handicap and inner beauty, while also foreshadowing his death. The final image of Doodle laying dead in his brother's arms, blood dripping from his mouth, aligns perfectly with the image of the scarlet bird that had succumbed to the winds of a hurricane earlier in the story. The story ends exactly how it foreshadowed it would. What "The Scarlet Ibis" lacks in length and character development as a short story, makes up for with its strong imagery, characterization, climactic ending, and theme.

One final note: Don't allow your resolution to drag. If your reader has made it to the end of your story, be aware that this is no longer your story. It is your reader's, and the resolution is the handoff of ownership. Leave your reader a clear hint as to its meaning, but the final decoding of your story's meaning is your reader's privilege, which is why you should not beat your reader over the head with explicitness. Your resolution should communicate in symbolism, brevity, and symmetry.

## EXAMPLE outline of "Regret":

*E. Resolution*

1. *In the final seconds as he falls to his death, Clint finds himself thinking about his life and how he might as well be honest with himself, for once, in his dying moment.*
2. *He tells himself that he has been wrong about everything and imagines his wife and daughter alone with the stalker. He realizes that his wife and daughter are probably in mortal danger. And he alone is to blame.*
3. *Final image: Clint falling to his death...without a word.*

## Now Write:

Review the thematic statement you wrote from the first week. Does your resolution highlight your theme? Does it force your reader to connect the final dots of thematic meaning? Will it leave your reader thinking about your story long after reading it? Outline your resolution when you have figured out a brief, symbolic, and fitting end to your story.

# DAY 14

## Revise Your Outline

One of the reasons you need to spend at least a week outlining is to give yourself time to view your story from a 30,000 foot perspective and notice its movement like a river. Does it follow a single, riveting path? Does it ebb and flow in a pleasing way? This is the time to uproot everything that gets in the way of its central conflict and meaning. Assume your reader will get confused if the story moves too fast. Asume your reader will get bored if it moves too slow. Shorten the less interesting parts and expand where your story has the most potential.

A story is also like a machine that engineers an emotional experience. No one wants to see the gears exposed. And certainly no one wants to hear gears grind. Revise your outline until the gears move one another in the planned direction and that each event has been set up to have the right amount of emotional leverage.

Other questions to consider as you revise your outline:

- Do you give your reader a reason to like the protagonist?

- Is exposition limited to brief moments that don't take readers out of your story?

- Are your characters' motives clear?

- Is your outline balanced—the middle longer than the beginning and end?

Keep in mind, an outline gives you the freedom to play with the story, to chisel it until you have a truly inspiring structure. It allows you to write your story in 2D and control its pacing and avoid the big mistakes that would otherwise require extensive revisions if you simply jumped into the rough draft.

## Now Write:

Revise your outline. Make sure it is cohesive and tight. If you ever divert from your protagonist's personal journey of hardship, challenge, and change, you need to be sure it adds to the story and doesn't last any longer than need be. Your reader will go only where your protagonist goes, so take out anything that doesn't add to his/her story arc.

# Wrap up of Week 2

## Can your outline sustain a novella or novel?

Before moving on to the drafting process, it is time to make an important decision. If you have been on the fence about whether to turn your outline into a short story, novella, or novel, you need to examine the potential of your outline. The problem with a short work of fiction is that you only have so much time to bring your story to life. If your characters do not have the time and space to develop, then you need to begin scaffolding your outline to sustain the length of a longer story. How long that story is depends upon the height of your protagonist's story arc.

For example, Tolkien's "Lord of the Rings" trilogy, Frodo Baggins could not have turned into a hero overnight, or a single book. Home-bound creatures like Hobbits struggle with stepping outside of the comfort of the Shire, much less a daring adventure to save the known world. It took many obstacles, life-and-death experiences, friends, mentors, and enemies to shape Frodo into the Hobbit who would take on Sauron and venture to Mt. Doom through an orc-ridden landscape.

However, our example "Regret" does not require a lengthy narrative to develop a character like Clint. He is arrogant and selfish, and his story arc is limited. But I've also had the opposite experience where I shortchanged a character's development simply because the story was no more than 5,400 words. In it, a young boy attends the funeral of his uncle but refuses to believe that the corpse in a casket is actually him. He spends the rest of the story trying to solve the mystery of what really happened to his favorite uncle, Rayne. My problem was that a character can't solve a mystery, much less the mystery of mortality, in 5,400 words. So I developed it into a novella ten years later.

If you are anything like me when I attempted to resurrect my writing career—many unfinished or unrealized novels—a novella is an effective confidence-booster. The length is not intimidating, though long enough to be called a book (and allow you to shatter that glass ceiling).

To do so, continue building your outline to support 20,000 to 50,000 words, or even a novel at 60,000 to 90,000 words. The purpose of this guide, however, is not to help you navigate the challenges of writing a book, but to equip you with the basic writing routines and practices that will enable you to write stories of any length for the rest of your life.

## Now Write:

If you think your story will work as a novella, or maybe even a novel, do not move onto the drafting process. Instead, spend the next week expanding your outline, developing the parts where additional characters, conflicts, and settings support the subplot f your story and immerse the reader in your protagonist's world. If, however, you feel like expanding your outline would draw things out, keep the story short and powerful.

# Week 3: The Rough Draft

## Introduction

You have lived and worked as a writer for two weeks and have many pages of brainstorming and detailed outlining, but your story is only a theory, a recipe, a game plan. Now it is game time.

The next seven days of exercises are going to feel different than the first fourteen. You will be making artistic decisions, avoiding major writing errors, and expanding your tool belt, but it's even more important that you continue writing each day even if you fall behind schedule—*especially* if you fall behind schedule. Nothing less than your daily habit of writing will manifest the story—and, more importantly, the writer—in you.

### How Many Words a Day?

How do you know if you are being productive as you sit down to write? The question is how many words can you muster on average on a slow day for your writing session? This low average will provide you a realistic baseline for planning out the completion of your rough draft. If you have no idea what to shoot for, 300 words is a good number—about one page typed. Consider this: If you write 300 words a day, six days a week for 52 weeks (a year), you will produce 93,600 words total, or roughly the length of a long novel. Obviously, you will have set-backs and days off, but even accounting for those, a consistent production of words per day and week will result in many published books throughout your life.

# Don't Sacrifice Your Soul

This is probably as good a time as any to point out that even as you establish a strong writing routine, you need to maintain a balanced lifestyle with enough exercise, sleep, and relationships so that you do not starve your soul. As stated above, you don't need an excessive amount of time to write. 30 to 40 minutes of focused, inspired writing is suitable *if* it is habitual and doesn't take away from the essentials of your life. A writer is going to feel more productive, more fueled in the margins of a happy life than spending hours on-end writing thousands of words a day in a life devoid of sustenance, love, and joy. It is better to write anonymously and produce a book on an annual or semi-annual basis than live miserably trying to force a dream.

# Next:

Divide up your outline into seven days of work. If this is a short story that is within 1,500 to 7,000 words, then you can divide up the story into seven parts. While you can go faster or slower, it is a good idea to make goals for each day. If this is a novella or novel, you can focus on the first 2 or 3 chapters. Or you might be more focused on a daily word count, especially if you are pressed for time. For either strategy, set a goal for each of the next seven days. Be specific, realistic, but also challenge yourself.

*In addition*, we suggest you make a journal entry after each day of writing. Even if you skip a day of working on your rough draft, for whatever reason, still make a journal entry. You need to continually reflect on your life as a writer—to hold yourself accountable and encourage yourself. Reflect on anything getting in the way of your routine or storytelling. More than just a writer, you need to become your own encourager, critic, and taskmaster.

# DAY 15

## Point of View

We have not discussed point of view up until now because, as a narrative device, it is not meant to draw attention to itself at all and can, for that reason, be taken for granted. Additionally, the strength of your story should not hinge on the POV you use...as long as you don't make any big mistakes.

To illustrate the pros and cons of each POV, we will revise a single passage from "Regret" multiple times. This part of the story finds Clint meeting Sheila, the character who provides one distraction too many on his quest of self-improvement. You will notice how each POV has a different effect and why the preferable POV—the third-person limited—is less distracting than the others.

### First-Person POV

Stay away from first-person in your early work, or until you master the basics of storytelling. A first-person narrator requires you to bring your protagonist to life while simultaneously mastering his/her voice and establishing the right level of reliability for your story. The other challenging aspect of the first-person POV is that there is no suspense about whether the protagonist lives or dies—if that is an important aspect of your plot.

**Our advice:** For these reasons, delay this point of view for later stories.

### EXAMPLE:

*I entered the Zen Cafe with a throbbing caffeine-addict's headache. Gurgling fountains of stale water and New Age music did little to soothe the pain or raise my hopes that this place offered anything stronger than a*

*Chai tea when I needed a triple shot mocha. I approached the display of the tea cakes behind glass and couldn't help but look around and remark on the fact that the 15 or so patrons did not talk or make a peep...That's when I noticed her: In the corner of the room sat a beautiful woman reading a book. No, she wasn't just beautiful. Stunning. And alone? What were the chances on a day when I literally had a moment to kill? My headache lifted and heart raced.*

## Analysis:

The benefit of a first-person narrator is giving the reader exclusive access to a protagonist's personal thoughts. The problem with first-person is that when a protagonist is constantly telling us his/her thoughts, they can get in the way of the story. The inexperienced writer may lose track of how often a protagonist's thoughts interrupt a story's flow.

## 2nd Person POV

The book you are reading is written from the second-person point of view, much like any manual, speaking directly to the reader. In fiction, second-person is an oddity outside of choose-your-own-adventure books.

**Our advice**: Avoid second-person most, if not all, of the time.

## EXAMPLE:

*I walked into the Zen cafe with a splitting headache: you know, the kind that punishes you for missing your daily dose of caffeine. Have you been in a place like this before? The bubbling fountains and New Age music made me wonder if they served anything besides Chai tea—maybe good enough for you, but I needed a multi-shot mocha to do the trick. That's when I saw her: a beautiful woman sitting at a small table in the corner. She was stunning and alone as if waiting for someone like you or me to just walk up and sweep her off her feet. What would you do in this situation? First of all, don't pass up the opportunity. You might crash and burn, but some things are worth public humiliation, and I couldn't pass up the risk.*

## *Analysis:*

Second-person narration pulls a reader out of the spell of storytelling, bringing attention to you, the reader, rather than the events that are unfolding. One of the reasons we read is so that we don't have to think about ourselves, to project our feelings onto other characters and watch them struggle and navigate challenges. The goal of a narrator is to immerse us in a story, not act like we are part of the story. So don't use second-person...unless you have a perfectly strange idea that just might work!

## 3rd Person Omniscient POV

The omniscient third-person is outdated and impersonal and a relic of the classic writers, jumping in and out of various characters' heads without showing favoritism, jolting the narrative to and fro. An omniscient POV is counterintuitive to a reader's desire to identify with a protagonist, intended to achieve a more objective telling of a story. An omniscient narrator lends itself to a story on a far grander scale with a historical perspective.

**Our advice**: Until you have mastered the third-person *limited* POV (in the next section) and have a specific artistic reason for using this one, avoid it.

## EXAMPLE:

*Clint entered the Zen Cafe with a headache due to caffeine withdrawal and worried the bubbling water and New Age music equaled a menu limited to Chai tea and mineral water. He knew what he needed—a triple shot mocha—and walked to the counter displaying bite-sized baked goods, most of which were green or marbled with various tea flavors when he a noticed a woman sitting at the table in the corner of the cafe. He stopped, unashamed, and stared. What was the coincidence that such a beauty sat alone?*

*Sheila did not notice the man staring at her, at least not at first. After all, she had come to the Zen Cafe to escape the attention of men. The water fixtures, music, and books warded off an overt presence of testosterone, and, after her last relationship, she needed a sanctuary from the opposite sex.*

## *Analysis:*

While this example creates an interesting dynamic between the two characters, this is Clint's story, and not only would it take too much time to jump in and out of both characters' heads, it would take away from the mystery and tension.

## 3rd Person Limited POV

In the third person limited POV, the narrator is outside of the story, narrating only the protagonist's experiences, thoughts, and emotions without meta-interruption. If there is action happening in another setting without the main character, the reader only learns about it from other characters. Because third-person limited is so close the protagonist, the author might find it difficult to resist commenting on the action. For example, I might be tempted to say, "Clint looked like a disaster when he entered the cafe," but the job of third person limited is to describe what is happening, not commenting on it.

Technically speaking, you can switch to another character's perspective in a short story, novella, or novel to reveal what is happening at another location from another key character's perspective; however, do this sparingly. Some novels will alternate perspectives from chapter to chapter, but this is rare in short stories. In our own example story, we switch perspectives at the end of the story when the ex-wife is confronted with the stalker and Clint is hiking with his new girlfriend.

**Our advice**: Use most of the time.

## EXAMPLE:

*Clint entered the Zen cafe for the first time, head pounding with caffeine withdrawal. He approached the counter of tea-flavored bakery goods and hoped to find something stronger than Chai tea. Except for the New Age music, bubbling fountains, and cafe machinery pulverizing drink ingredients, there was no noise. He looked around to the dozen or so patrons to see if anyone was talking—wondering if speaking was allowed—when he saw her: a slender woman in a purple knit wrap, huddled with a book...alone.*

*Though he could not take in the full picture of her countenance, he could tell she was within a few years of his own age and devastatingly beautiful. Clint felt his headache lift...replaced by a shortness of his breath and a racing heart. He needed to talk to her, get her number, or just fail in the attempt because he could not live with himself if he let the vision of his future happiness just sit there undisturbed.*

## *Analysis:*

The above example is the quickest, smoothest of the examples because it focuses on narrating the events from Clint's perspective and describes what he sees, feels, and thinks as if in real time. However, it does not share *every* thought that passes through his mind, but screens the most relevant thoughts; it does not draw attention to the reader or the narrator; and it does not slow the story down by jumping into another character's perspective.

## Psychic Distance

Psychic distance is the emotional distance between the reader and the protagonist. Before you start writing from a specific POV for your story, it is important to first understand something that is far more important than any of the POV you choose: do not artificially create emotional distance between you and your reader. Whichever POV you decide on for your story, use it to share what your protagonist is thinking and feeling. We, as readers, should not feel the same distance from your protagonist as other characters feel. When your protagonist hurts, we need to hurt. When your protagonist feels alone, we need to hear the thoughts of abandonment. When your protagonist overcomes a challenge, we need to experience the unbearable weight lift from their soul.

Read the example below for intentional psychic distance:

*Clint entered the Zen cafe for the first time, head pounding. Except for the New Age music, bubbling fountains, and cafe machinery pulverizing drink ingredients, there was no noise. He looked around and saw a slender woman in a purple knit wrap, huddled with a book...alone. Clint felt his headache lift. He decided he would have to talk to her and get her number, or at least fail in the attempt.*

Notice that we don't experience how his world stops at the sight of the woman as we did in prior examples. On the other hand, you will notice that the passage reads quicker and gets to the point faster. There will be times in your story that you need to hurry things along—transitory scenes that do not require access to your protagonist's every emotion. When you increase psychic distance, the story will move faster, but don't do this unless pacing is more important than emotional connection at that point.

## Now Write:

Write the opening paragraph of your story in the third-person limited POV, and then try out a second option for fun if you have time. You might be surprised at how different the story reads or how natural one POV might feel for your story than another one.

After choosing which one you like the most, revise it by eliminating emotional distance. Where can you describe more acutely what your protagonist thinks or feels?

# DAY 16

## Start Fast

As you continue your draft, push past the fear of imperfection, trust your outline, and just tell the story. Even if your story makes it into the hands of other readers, no one is going to care about your wording so long as it does NOT get in the way of your story. The narration should be a glass pane—to show your story as clearly as possible. That is it. Anything else is curtains and window dressing. It is easy to get hung up on style, trends, or techniques. Instead, focus on telling the story. Don't try to sound like anyone else. Don't imitate another writer. Don't overthink the wording. Be a storyteller. And dig into the story right away.

Here is an example of the opening scene of "Regret":

*The rock should have given way by now. It held all a hundred and ninety two pounds of Clint's weight, providing the only friction between him and a sedimentary floor seventy feet below. This was supposed to be a mind-clearing trip—a chance for Clint to stretch the fibers of his muscles before soaking them later in a hot tub at a 4-star resort. He needed to unscrew his mind with isolation and expensive wine, but a realization anchored his final thoughts as he dug his fingertips into the rock: I have wasted my life.*

While your outline provides a strong structure—intrigue, conflict, and theme—the first paragraphs needs to over-deliver. If your outline's description of the opening scene sounds suspenseful, your actual narration needs to have a physiological effect on your reader, turning black and white symbols into bio-electric currents. The above paragraph starts with the imminent likelihood of death; in fact, there seems to be no other plausible outcome. Details about the climb and resort provide a brief glimpse into his character—that he is stressed, lonely, and only focused on himself. By the end of the opening paragraph, it goes straight to the heart of the story's theme: his entire life has been a waste and now it seems too late to do anything about it.

While the purpose of your opening paragraphs need to establish character, setting, and theme, they should ultimately make it impossible for your reader to put the story down, which means you don't include a single wasteful word or detail.

## Slowing down time

Don't waste true suspense. When you have your reader gripping the book (or electronic device) and cannot look away, slow the narrative down. Dwell in the suspense. Movies do this literally by using slow motion, sometimes slowing seconds into milliseconds with special effects. You can do this effectively in writing by describing every little detail of the suspenseful scene. The more you describe, the slower time goes, the bigger the build up, and more suspenseful the scene. The opening scene of "Regret" spends a paragraph that describes what happens in only seconds.

## Speeding up time

While you want to slow down the most interesting, gripping parts of your story, you do not want to dwell on anything the reader doesn't need to know or would be boring to describe. To skip the boring details, summarize what happens in chunks. BUT DO NOT DO THIS IN THE OPENING SCENE. Everything in the opening scene needs to happen as if it is happening now (which does not mean it should be present tense). Refrain from "telling" almost anything in the opening scene. In the first draft of "Regret," we gave additional details about his work stress and the resort in which he was staying, but that slowed down the pace of my opening scene too much, so we revised it and took out nearly all exposition.

You can also literally speed up the reading experience, or pace, by writing short, choppy sentences. Short sentences read quickly. They create a sense of urgency. Things happen fast in fewer words.

Do this in bursts when you want the movement of your sentences to mirror quick action in your scene. But do not go on for too long. Short, choppy writing gets old fast.

## Now Write:

Review your opening scene and make sure that it reads quickly. Continue this quick pace through the introduction of your inciting incident.

# DAY 17

## Show, Don't Tell

Novice writers often spend the beginning of the story telling exposition, describing the setting, and telling characters' backstories because they assume if readers don't understand everything at once they will be confused and abandon the story. The contrary is actually more true: most readers abandon a story out of boredom or the lack of forward momentum. They only care about what is happening if something is actually happening!

Be careful with exposition. It is easy to begin inserting it out of a lack of trust in your reader. If you focus on moving the story forward, showing your protagonist's conflict worsen paragraph by paragraph, readers will follow you to the end. However, if you go backwards in time a few paragraphs in a short story—or chapters in a novel—your readers might forget why they picked up the story in the first place.

One way to test if you are showing or telling is to ask yourself a simple question about each paragraph: What is happening? If the answer to this question is the character is thinking about doing something, reflecting on his/her past, explaining the setting, flashing back to a different time, or describing a character's emotions, then you are "telling," not "showing." However, if your current paragraph shows your character interacting with other characters as a result of the main conflict, then you are "showing."

So when is it a good time for exposition? Keep in mind that readers do not read for info dumps. If there is no other way to explain why something is happening, then let your reader discover it with your protagonist because readers have built-in exposition detectors and too much 'plot-speak' will dampen the illusion.

## Conflict is Key and Cliché is Poison

Conflict captures our attention. Whether it is a fight on the street, an argument in the next room, or a relationship breakup, we can hardly resist paying attention to people going at each other. Perhaps it is the human race's history of tribalism, the need to band together and protect ourselves from enemies—or attacking them before they attack us. Whatever the reason, conflict wakes us up out of the fog of boredom and mundanity. The advice here has less to do with your overall plot and more about finding a conflict in every situation, even if it is finding a way to get from one part of your outline to the other in an interesting way.

In the Zen Cafe example of "Regret," we had to figure out a way for Clint to meet Sheila and did not have time to integrate her character slowly into the story, but at the same time we didn't want to use a common cliche, such as having him bump into her at a random location and have him apologize as he picks up her things and looks at her face to face. How many times have you seen that exact thing in movies and TV? (I've seen it happen twice in two of the past five movies I've most recently watched.) In "Regret," we avoid such a cliche by placing Clint in a cafe he's never frequented, but in order to place him there we created a minor conflict: Clint woke up that morning to discover that he was out of coffee; then, after breakfast, he went to his usual coffee stop only to find a long line. By this point he has a caffeine headache and was forced to walk across the street to the Zen Cafe out of desperation, finding himself in a place that made him feel like a fish out of water—a small but interesting tension.

If two characters are working together to solve a problem, don't depict them congratulating each other and patting one another on the back. Show them arguing vehemently about each other's ideas, every step of the way, even if they are partners or friends. It is far more engaging.

## Now Write:

As you connect the dots from the first part of your outline to your second, use conflict, tension, curiosity. Whenever you transition to any part, do not allow the tension or curiosity to slack.

# DAY 18

## Dialogue Conventions

We could write a book exclusively about dialogue, but you'd be better served by simply reading novels and paying attention to the ebb and flow of their dialogue. However, all competent writers should be aware of a few basic rules. We have avoided discussing writing mechanics as much as possible because we assume you are bringing a basic grasp of literary skills to the table, otherwise you wouldn't be this serious about developing a writing career. But I have suffered through a Masters program of creative writing with 'educated' writers who lacked a basic grasp of writing conventions, including dialogue, and it's only fair to you to address, briefly, the major technical and stylistic mistakes to avoid when writing dialogue.

## <u>Dialogue Topic 1: Formatting</u>

Whenever a character speaks, start a new paragraph. When characters go back and forth, this should be a new paragraph:

*"What are you reading?" Clint asked the woman who ignored him as he approached her table.*

*"Something more enlightening than a conversation with a stranger," the woman answered without looking up from her book, though she took the time to take a sip of her mug. "At least so far."*

*"A good conversation," he chuckled, "beats a good book any day. That's my experience, anyway."*

This dialogue goes back and forth between characters, so each character's response gets a new paragraph. Stick within the same paragraph until you switch to a new character's response.

## <u>Dialogue Topic 2: Punctuation and quotation marks</u>

Once I read an entire novel where the punctuation marks were outside of quotation marks rather than inside. It wasn't a bad novel, but it wasn't the best either—surprise, surprise. The point is, punctuation goes inside of quotation marks:

*"What are you reading?" asked Clint.*

Also, when you interrupt a character with attribution, only use a comma, not a period, after the attribution:

*"A good conversation,"* **he chuckled,** *"beats a good book any day."*

The word 'beats' is not capitalized because the attribution interrupts the character's thought. The thought or sentence is not over until after the word *day*. But if your character finishes a thought, then use a period after the attribution:

*"A good conversation beats a good book any day,"* **he said.** *"That's my experience, anyway."*

## <u>Dialogue Topic 3: Using and not using 'said'</u>

New writers often take the advice of their high school writing teachers too seriously when they say to vary their word choice, to find more expressive words to replace *said* in dialogue, such as *explained*, *declared*, *expressed*, *exclaimed*, etc. Unless your character actually mumbles, shouts, whines, sneers, cackles, laughs, bellows, or cries out, stick with *said* because it keeps the focus on the characters' dialogue rather than on the narrator.

If you have two characters going back and forth, it is fine *not* to use dialogue attribution...to an extent:

*Sheila opened his closet and squinted at the heap of shoes and sporting equipment.*

*"Clint, do you have good shoes for hiking?"*

*"Sure. Why?"*

*"There is one section of the hike where your life will depend on it."*

*"I bought them from an outdoor equipment store this spring."*

*"Perfect."*

In the example above, it is clear who is talking back and forth; thus, using *said* every time would sound redundant. However, the reader can get lost without attribution if it goes on too long, which is a stylistic error referred to as 'talking heads,' so only omit attribution in short bursts.

## <u>Dialogue Topic 4: Characterization</u>

Characterization is the method by which you bring your characters to life. If you remember from your high school freshman English class, direct characterization is when you tell your reader directly what to think of your character, such as,

*Sheila was self-confident and wary of men she didn't know.*

This is 'telling' rather than 'showing,' and is not as effective as direct characterization which would show Sheila acting self-confident and wary of men:

*Clint looked around the cafe and saw a slender woman in a purple knit wrap, huddled with a book...alone. Clint felt his headache lift. He decided he would have to talk to her and get her number, or at least fail in the attempt.*

*"What are you reading?" Clint asked the woman who ignored him as he approached her table.*

**"Something more enlightening than a conversation with a stranger," the woman answered.**

Sheila's response shows she is confident, self-possessed, and wary of men through her words. Now tack on a description to the attribution and—*voila!*—we have an even more precise characterization:

*"Something more enlightening than a conversation with a stranger," the woman answered* **bringing her mug to her lips and taking the time to sipped to satisfaction without eye contact.**

At the same time, be careful not to get carried away and constantly interrupt your dialogue with too many details and descriptions. My high school writing teacher pointed out on many occasions that I made this very mistake, delving into descriptive passages of a character's thoughts or physical attributes in the middle of dialogue, totally derailing the flow. The reader is going to be more interested in what characters say to one another, like we would if we were eavesdropping on an argument between two people we know. Yes, it's important to know if someone slams a fist while speaking, or backs away, or avoids eye contact, or sips coffee. However, don't break the spell of your readers' experience by getting in their way.

## Dialogue Topic 5: Being Cliché

Our brains are wired to use the path of least resistance, constantly on battery-saving mode and conserving energy for real crises; in other words, we are wired to think lazily. A lazy writer's brain wants to use the same old cliche and overused dialogue. Just look at the way Hollywood writers recycle the same old lines over and over again, such as "It's complicated," or "I'm walking here!" or "Say hello to my little friend!"

Why would you want to remind the audience of other people's movies? Other characters' dialogue? Why would you want your characters to sound like you are just inserting phrases from ChatGPT?

To write fresh dialogue, avoid using the first thing that comes to your mind and *instead* use the first thing that would come from *your character's mind*. In other words, your characters should sound like themselves in each scene, and if you don't know your characters enough to know how they talk, their go-to euphemisms, the region from where they are from, the extent of their vocabulary, or pet phrases, you need to spend more time brainstorming your characters. Dialogue reveals a character's personality and experience. Don't shortchange your characters' quality because you aren't listening close enough to what *they* would say.

## Dialogue Topic 6: 'Plot-speak'

One of the most abused writing techniques we have briefly mentioned before is when the author info-dumps exposition using *plot-speak,* which is our term for dialogue that is used to provide any obvious plot information in a heavy-handed, obvious way—those times in a book or a movie when a character stops being a character and becomes a sign post for the plot.

When Sheila invites Clint to hike a local mountain, Sheila needs to hint that there is the possibility of danger. Using plot-speak as foreshadowing, we might have her say something like,

*"Do you have good shoes for hiking, Clint?"*

*"Sure. Why?"*

*"There is one section of the hike where your life will depend on it!"*

But this is too obvious and doesn't fit Sheila's thrill-seeking nature. She doesn't consider the hike a risk because it doesn't compare to the risks she really enjoys taking when given the opportunity. Also, this dialogue is implausible because she wouldn't want to scare Clint from going with her.

Stronger dialogue would sound more like this:

*"Do you have good shoes?" Sheila asked.*

*"Sure," Clint said without thinking.*

*"What kind?" she pressed him.*

*"Um, the kind you get from an outdoor equipment store. I spent at least two hundred dollars on them."*

*"How long ago?"*

*"This spring. Why?"*

*"Just so you have good footing," she said. "I don't need to carry you down the mountain if you roll your ankle!"*

While this dialogue exchange still draws attention to the fact that safety is going to be a concern on this hike, it stays true to Sheila's character without beating the reader over the head with obvious foreshadowing. A careful reader will notice the hint. A lazy reader might ignore it or just think it's odd for her to focus on shoes, but the dialogue sounds natural enough for the situation.

The same mistake can be made when attempting to take exposition shortcuts. An author might think he/she is avoiding slowing down a story with exposition by having a character explain important details, but this can pull readers out of the story as well. In "Regret," Clint has a long history of failing to follow through with responsibilities. We could use plot-speak to reveal this trait explicitly in a conversation with his ex-wife:

"I promise to help you move out this weekend," said Clint over the phone.

"Do you realize," returned his ex-wife, "that you never follow through with your responsibilities?"

"That's not true."

"I know it's true," she said, indignant. "I lived it for ten years!"

"I will be there to help. I promise."

"I don't believe you. But if by some miracle you do show up, you can tell that stalker to stay away from me."

"I will. You can count on me."

"Whatever."

The above dialogue exchange sounds less like real people and more like an author trying to hit the reader over the head with not-so-obvious hints about potential danger and Clint's irresponsibilty. Instead, here is a revised passage:

"I promise to help you this weekend," said Clint over the phone.

"Sure," said his ex-wife.

"No, I really mean it."

"You don't need to make any promises to me, Clint. That was kind of the point of the divorce."

"Yeah, yeah, I know," he said, defenceless. "But it's important to me to help. I will be there for you and Liz."

*"Well you know the time. If you did anything, you could at least knock on that creep's door and tell him to stay away. I'll have my baseball bat if you need it."*

*"You can count on it."*

*"Well, don't do it for me. Do it for Liz. My parents are out of town this weekend."*

*"I'm doing it for both of you."*

*"Okay."*

This dialogue exchange reveals Clint's ex-wife's lack of trust without being overly obvious, and it sounds more natural for the situation as the ex-married couple attempts to make amends.

## Now Write:

As you write today, focus on dialogue. Remember: Don't write the first thing that comes to your mind; write the first thing that would come to your characters' minds.

If you need to reveal exposition or foreshadowing in your dialogue, avoid *plot-speak*. Hint at details that reveal your characters' backgrounds without directly going into full length histories. More importantly, bring your characters to life through the words they say and how they say them.

# DAY 19

## Don't 'Tense' Up

This is a simple but important point to make: only use past tense. Once in a while, you will read a bestseller like "The Hunger Games" that effectively uses present tense, but if you master the basics of storytelling, you can break any rules you want for effect.

For beginners, developing writers, and even published ones, past tense is the go-to convention. Sometimes writers think present tense sounds more suspenseful as the action unfolds live, but not only is present tense rare in storytelling, we have been telling stories in the past tense for millennia, and our ears are tuned for it.

Most likely, you have chosen a tense to use already, but inexperienced writers often go back and forth between tenses unknowingly, and while verb tense has many subtle rules that your editor or proofreaders will help you correct, be sure you are consistently using the past verb tense to narrate your story.

## Word choice

If you reach for a thesaurus or look up synonyms online multiple times in a writing session, you have missed the point of word choice. Words are the building blocks of sentences to communicate visual pictures and ideas *clearly*. If you frequently use words you aren't comfortable using, then you are likely misusing their situational subtleties and thus communicating less clearly. Readers are never impressed with a writer's large vocabulary. They are impressed when something is written so clearly and naturally that they forget they are reading at all.

One of the lessons I learned before heading to college was to leave my thesaurus at home. (This was back in the days when you had physical copies of dictionaries and thesauruses cluttering up your desk). If you word-shop for every sentence, you are trying too hard. Focus on storytelling, not word-smithing. The only justifiable use of a thesaurus is when you have a word on the tip of your tongue and you need some help...extracting it.

## Nouns and verbs

If you build a brick wall, you use bricks and mortar. You do not use wood, glass, plastic, metal, or any other materials that threaten the integrity of the wall. In the same way, a story's narration should depend upon two tangible materials: nouns and verbs, the building blocks of images and actions. Inexperienced authors often feel insecure about whether or not readers are going to understand everything they are trying to show or say and often revert to adjectives, adverbs, or passive writing.

Don't write like this:

*Clint was a selfish man and only thought of himself. He was handsome if he took care of himself, but he didn't take care of himself. He certainly didn't care about people he didn't know. He angrily told people off if he thought they were being rude, and selfishly avoided spending time with his daughter, but not because he didn't love her. He loved her immensely. He just didn't take the time to show that he was a caring father.*

Did you count how many times adjectives and adverbs popped up? Let's look at that passage again and identify the obvious adverbs and adjectives:

*Clint was a <u>selfish</u> man and only thought of himself. He was <u>handsome</u> if he took care of himself, but he didn't take care of himself. He <u>certainly</u> didn't care about people he didn't know. He <u>angrily</u> told people off if he thought they were being <u>rude</u>, and <u>selfishly</u> avoided spending time with his* *daughter, but not because he didn't love her. He loved her <u>immensely</u>. He just didn't take the time to show that he was a <u>caring</u> father.*

Also, the above passage does not show action. It summarizes action passively. It does not actually show Clint acting in a 'selfish,' 'angry,' or 'caring' manner.

Instead, write like this:

*Clint didn't call his daughter that morning, even though it was Saturday and he was supposed to take her to the park. He was out of coffee and, by the time he showered and ate breakfast, his head pounded with caffeine withdrawal and so drove two miles to Mocha Moon, his favorite coffee stop.*

*He regretted his choice as soon as he walked in the door and stepped into the line that wound along the wall to the door.*

*"This is ridiculous," Clint said, thinking out loud.*

*"It's 9AM. What do you expect?" said the man in front of him, nearly a foot shorter and wearing a sport coat.*

*"I expect a cup of coffee while it's still morning," Clint shot back.*

*"This place is popular for a reason," said Mr. Sportcoat.*

*Clint looked down at the fellow caffeine addict, said, "I came here for coffee, not to be part of a popular scene," and then walked out the door.*

There are very few adjectives or adverbs in the above passage because it shows him in a specific situation acting both selfish and aggravated. Yes, it takes time to build with many layers of nouns and verbs, but that is storytelling. And it is far more fun to read.

## Passive vs Active Writing

One of the most simple pieces of writing advice is also one of the most abused: writing in the active voice. Active voice places the thing doing the action at the beginning of the sentence, followed by the action verb:

*Clint ran out the door and drove two miles to Mocha Moon.*

The mistake many writers make looks like the following:

*The Mocha Moose was two miles away and was the only place Clint could think of going.*

Grammatically speaking, the above sentence is fine, but stylistically it is awful. Clint is at the end of the sentence. The sentence begins with the indirect object, the Mocha Moose, followed by two uses of the linking verb 'was.' To help you avoid the confusion and slow pace of passive writing, avoid linking and helping verbs as much as possible in your narration.

For quick reference, here is a list of linking and helping verbs:

*is, am, was, were*

*be, being, been*

*may, might, must, can*

*shall, should, could, would, will*

*have, has, had, having*

*do, does, did*

Any time you can cut these from your writing, your writing improves. Instead, start your sentences with the person or thing doing the action and follow with action verbs. That is not to say your sentences should be devoid of variety—only that you focus on characters doing things, and that you construct your sentences in a likewise manner.

## Now Write:

Review your draft and start crossing out gratuitous adverbs and adjectives; revise as many passive sentences (and put the subject at the beginning of the sentence). If you find a passage that depends on adverbs and adjectives, rewrite it with action, concrete details, and language filled with nouns and verbs.

# DAY 20

## Make Your Story Feel Plausible

As a storyteller, your greatest challenge is making your readers forget they are reading, to engulf them with the journey of your protagonist in a world you have imagined. Of course complete immersion is impossible, but readers yearn for those moments of vicarious bliss in a good story, and the last thing you want to do is disrupt their stupor with implausibility.

Plausibility is not the same thing as realism, but rather your in-story logic that satisfies the reader's intrusive judgment. Keep in mind that a reader's judgment is always analyzing the consistency of a story's plausibility, or the rules of its reality. We don't expect your story to be a mirror of real life, but to feel 'real' while taking us away to a different world with established rules.

We are not going to discuss obvious plausibility problems, for example, an out-of-shape 'office guy' who suddenly displays kickboxing skills and takes on a street gang by himself. Rather, we assume you have the common sense to strike a good balance between genre tropes and plausibility. But there are more subtle variables that can impact plausibility as well.

## Genre Plausibility

Every genre has its own free passes on reality, such as intergalactic space travel in a space opera. Space travel is a sci-fi genre plausibility, and readers expect such stories to be filled with spaceships that can warp, jump to light speed, or slip through time-bending worm holes. Nobody worries about how time passes much quicker for those the spaceships leave behind. Not only does space travel comes with sci-fi territory, but any attempt to make it more realistic, or to ask too many questions about it, would turn the fan base off.

However, outside of your genre's acceptable free passes, the rest of your story's world needs to be grounded in a recognizable reality. As you layer your setting in description and show your characters reacting and navigating the events of your plot, make sure that your characters talk and act like real people. The less human your characters act—even stock characters—the less 'real' your story will feel, especially when you expect your readers to suspend their belief in other ways.

Here are examples of other plausibility free passes:

Action/adventure: *the flesh wound*. It is perfectly acceptable that your protagonist sustains at least one wound that would debilitate an actual human being but in an action/adventure story only requires a brief rest and bandage. Such flesh wounds would cause us a trip to the hospital, antibiotics, and possibly surgery. But a hero can keep marching on. To balance out the medical magic of a bandage, there should physical limitations that do cause problems for the hero.

Mystery: *the convenient clue*. At some point the detective or investigator in a mystery finds the right clue in the right place at the right time...at the exact same moment before something bad happens. Typically, a mystery story's strength is the very difficult task of solving clues, so the occasional convenient clue is a break for the protagonist and the reader.

Thriller: *the unsuspecting bad guy*. While living a dual identity is not easy for just anyone, it comes easier for psychopaths—the antagonists of thrillers. Not only is the psychopath usually unknown in a thriller, but is often the most likable and harmless character in the whole story until his/her true identity is revealed. However, if this is the bad guy in every thriller, or if multiple villains in a thriller are chameleons, then it becomes a hallow trick.

To balance out the free passes of whatever your genre is, be sure the rules of physics and nature apply to all of the non-genre elements of your story. Though intergalactic space travel is an accepted technology in science fiction, it is still a mechanical technology that is subject to fuel issues and the laws of thermodynamics. Even a star cruiser should break down once in a while.

## Plausible Tone

Even if you stay within the lines of you genre rules, you can still destroy plausibility without awareness of tone. Tone is the emotion your narrator shows towards your characters and the world in which they exist. If your narrator's underlying emotion toward your protagonist is sarcastic, it not only creates a greater psychic distance between the reader and the character, it also establishes a certain type of plausibility compared to a story with a more sincere tone. A sarcastic narrator creates the likelihood that bad things will happen:

*Clint clung to the rock, grasping for dear life—as if his life was in fact 'dear' and added any of value to the universe.*

The above example's narrator clearly does not care about Clint, so it is very plausible that if he doesn't die now, he will likely at some point.

*Clint grasped the rock with all his strength. Could this be the end? Would he feel his bones break and life escape his grasp? He was too young. Too able bodied. Too innocent of any great crimes against the universe to deserve this kind of end.*

The above example's tone is emotionally close to Clint's perspective, almost inseparable. This establishes a more sympathetic set of rules for the story. This tone forces the reader to feel sorry for Clint, thus making it more plausible that not only will he survive, but likely find redemption by story's end.

*Clint grasped the rock which jiggled and toyed with his grasp. The mountain found nothing forgiving or likable about the man clinging to its mineral scabs for dear life and should have shrugged him off immediately, so poor was its impression of his soul. And yet it heard him cry out—a miserable but honest cry to have a second chance to right his wrongs. Being a mountain made of rock and mineral and sand that had seen the dawn of time, it thought little of his plea bargaining with the universe and left him hanging.*

This example has a satirical narrator, imbibing the mountain with more soul and value than the human character clinging to it. Not only does a satiric tone set up humorous events, it also makes a more ridiculous plot plausible.

The tone we actually chose for "Regret" is both objective and close to Clint's thoughts and emotions without much commentary...mostly.

As previously shown, below is the opening paragraph. Do you see any commentary or evidence of an attitude from my narrator?

*The rock should have given way by now. It held all a hundred and ninety two pounds of Clint's weight, providing the only friction between him and a sedimentary floor seventy feet below. This was supposed to be a mind-clearing trip—a chance for Clint to stretch the fibers of his muscles before soaking them later in a hot tub at a 4-star resort. He needed to unscrew his mind with isolation and expensive wine, but a like the small embedded rock that impossibly held his weight, a single thought anchored his final thoughts: 'I wasted my life.'*

Two sentences display surprise that Clint is still alive at this moment: *"The rock should have given way by now,"* and *"the small embedded rock that impossibly held his weight."* The words *'should'* and *'impossibly'* show the narrator has an opinion or feeling about the fact Clint hasn't fallen yet. The tone is a bit on the curious side, finding amusement in Clint's predicament.

The point is to be aware of the tone you are using so that you don't write a sarcastic-sounding story that is meant to be serious, or vice versa. Even worse is when your narrator makes conflicting tonal commentaries through a story, making for a difficult mess to fix. We suggest that you do not comment on what is happening unless you are going for a very specific tone or style of narration.

As you continue working on your story, novella, or novel, you may feel that the tone you use should be the last of your worries. After all, you are settling into the life of a writer with a committed routine. You are producing written pages on a consistent basis. You are wielding the tools of narration like a craftsman. Why should you worry about one of the more abstract concepts as tone?

Because at this point in your writing process you can handle 'talking shop.' Maybe you won't master tone in this narrative venture, but you never will until you start somewhere. The lazy writer doesn't pay attention to tone. Even professional writers often sacrifice tone to indulge implausible plot fireworks. But just because you are less experienced than other writers doesn't mean you have to write like one.

## Now Write:

Finish your story. Be consistent in tone and account for plausibility.

# Day 21

## Bringing it all Together

With so many story elements at play as you write, which one demands the most attention in your rough draft? Plot? Character? Theme? Tone?Everything in a story boils down to one thing, and one thing only: your protagonist's struggle to overcome challenges. When you write, you are writing an experience for your readers to live vicariously through the eyes of your main character. So make it dangerous, heartbreaking, and inspiring. Let them know what it feels like to overcome the extraordinary. Or simply remind them of the struggle and resilience of being human.

Focus on your protagonist's struggle the entire story, not letting up until he/she has earned the resolution that you have outlined. Readers want to feel better about life after reading a story or book—to be left with the echoes of great courage and survival whispering in their imagination as they face the chaos and mundanity of everyday life.

## What Happens if You Stray From Your Outline?

Sometimes the drafting process takes you in a different direction than your outline, and this shouldn't worry you because this is *your* story, *your* novella, *your* book, and you should not limit yourself by creating artificial barriers for yourself. If you discover a better story buried in your brainstorming and outlining, then go for it. Just be sure to consult your own writing advice. Review your notes and outline and figure out why you constructed your story the way you did. It's possible that your new changes work even better, but they may create narrative inconsistencies if you stick with your overall plot. Decisions like this and their cascading consequences are all part of the creative process—the messy, unpredictable side of writing that either inspires you or sends you looking for a new hobby (because it is not just a hobby).

In summary, the quality of your writing will be reflected by the quality of your writing process. If you give your writing process enough time, structure, logic, and creative freedom—if you give greater precedence and importance to the process than you do the actual words you write—then you will grow every day you write.

Every great author is buried beneath a certain number of rough drafts, marked-up manuscripts, and failed attempts. No one can tell you how many words, how many pages, how many drafts, how many stories or books it takes to unearth the great author in you. You will make this discovery on your own, but the most important thing is not how your writing improves over time with the right habits; it is that *you* have changed in the process.

# After 3 Weeks: Your True Identity

If you followed this process with fidelity, even if you tailored it to your own style, then you have lived and worked as a writer for 21 days and produced a full or partial draft of a manuscript that is now a signpost of the future. What you do next is inconsequential to the fact that you have made a fundamental change in your life.

Take a break, breathe, and give yourself a chance to take stock of your progress. You have done more than just produce a story or a couple chapters. You have established yourself as a writer. The next step is to solidify this lifestyle and, in the next three week cycle, continue your routine as you edit or continue your story. The scope of this book is not to help you with developmental editing or professional proofreading, which you can be outsourced to many online services without breaking the bank. But once you have a completed and polished draft, you can do whatever best fits your goals—self-publishing, traditional publishing, or both—because now it's not a matter of *if* you become a published writer, but *when*.

Perhaps just as remarkable are the other changes you notice in your life, such as feeling bored in the midst of doing activities you once found stimulating because no other hobby, cognitive challenge, or source of entertainment will be as satisfying as writing. You will watch a movie, but it won't immerse you the same way. You'll attend a play, but wish you were back home writing one yourself. You'll listen to an album, but only hear the soundtrack of a future story to write. When you plan your next vacation, you won't be looking forward to tropical beaches or tourist excursions, but the hours of unimpeded writing at your disposal.

You have begun more than a story or even a career. You have manifested new habits. And in time they will be your legacy.

# Epilogue

## The Motivation Myth

At any point in this 21-day journey, and certainly after it, you might find yourself struggling with motivation. Motivation is the thing that stirs our brain from stasis to activity, from decline to growth, from status quo to improvement. And while it takes very little to discourage us from something as ambitious as developing the life of a writer, it seems to require great levels of motivation to sustain such a life. But why? Why can't we just do the hard things that take us to our goals? Why do we have to be motivated to carve out extra time each day to the very thing we should be motivated to do? Why can't we just write the book we've been dreaming about writing for years?

Ironically, we have the incentive to put in the time and effort to write every day, so why do we struggle with motivation when we actually try to?

Our brains are wired to follow the path of least resistance as much as possible. The brain is the 'organ' of the body that requires the most amount of energy to function, thus burning the greatest number of calories. The brain's ability to live in extremes—to go from multitasking to zoning out—shows that what usually prompts us to action, or what motivates us, are extreme emotions: survival, fear, deadlines, ambition, greed, anxiety, threats, desires, passions, and needs. But we don't live in a constant state of these high-level motivators, thankfully, and when we get a moment to relax we usually choose a passive way to spend our time to decompress and often settle into a stream of passivity for hours at a time.

Urgent activities rescue us from meaninglessness, and passive entertainment rescues us from the weariness of urgency. And so the cycle goes on. We are usually too busy dealing with the urgent demands of our jobs, homes, relationships and needs to take any time to write. And when we have a moment to sit down in front of a computer, our brains are fried and require a break.

What if we don't have a way out of this unending cycle of cognitive dissonance? The easy answer seems to be the same problem: We are motivated to write but paradoxically lack the motivation to write when the rubber meets the road.

Even the figurative things of the universe follow the general rules of physics—the law of inertia snuffs out new endeavors and hobbies after a few weeks, or even days, just as a pencil will come to a stop after being pushed across a table.

Using the same principals that govern the physical universe, if you increase the velocity of an *project*, you will increase its momentum as well. But continued movement requires a renewing source of energy. You can only sustain a writing project if, after putting it into motion, you continue to fuel it with energy and work. The moment you stop exerting energy and work, momentum for that project will decrease. The 'thought' of writing a book does not create motivation. You create motivation by the act of writing itself. The more you write, the more you practice the habit, the more momentum your writing will have...and the more motivated you will be to continue writing daily.

If you engineer your time and your habits so that that energy is utilized efficiently; if you adjust your techniques as you go; if you apply the mechanism of routine to prompt you to write daily whether you like it or not—you will not only break away from the gravity of passivity, you will find yourself more motivated as you go.

Do not judge your potential success or identity as a writer based upon your varying levels of motivation. If you need the motivation to push through and see a novel to the end, then you need to put more time and energy into your project and overcome emotional resistance. You need to set goals that you can achieve that are progressively more ambitious. When gravity and inertia—when life itself—are holding you back from writing—that is when you need to write the most.

Write more, write often, and most importantly write when you are not motivated. Motivation apart from hard work and good habits is a myth. First manifest the will-power (a disciplined state of mind) to overcome the inertia of reality. Only then will the motivation manifest. But at that point you won't even need it.

www.ingramcontent.com/pod-product-compliance
Lightning Source LLC
Chambersburg PA
CBHW022202150726

47992CB00002B/924